Linguistic Theory
and Structural Stylistics

LANGUAGE AND COMMUNICATION LIBRARY

Series Editor: Roy Harris, University of Oxford

Vol 1. - MORRIS
  Saying and Meaning in Puerto Rico
Vol 2. - TAYLOR
  Linguistic Theory and Structural Stylistics

A Related Pergamon Journal

LANGUAGE & COMMUNICATION

An Interdisciplinary Journal

Editor: Roy Harris, *University of Oxford*

The primary aim of the journal is to fill the need for a publication forum devoted to the discussion of topics and issues in communication which are of interdisciplinary significance. It will publish contributions from researchers in all fields relevant to the study of verbal and non-verbal communication.

Emphasis will be placed on the implication of current research for establishing common theoretical frameworks within which findings from different areas of study may be accommodated and interrelated.

By focusing attention on the many ways in which language is integrated with other forms of communicational activity and interactional behaviour it is intended to explore ways of developing a science of communication which is not restricted by existing disciplinary boundaries.

*Free specimen copy available on request.

NOTICE TO READERS

Dear Reader

An invitation to Publish in and Recommend the Placing of a Standing Order to Volumes Published in this Valuable Series

If your library is not already a standing/continuation order customer to this series, may we recommend that you place a standing/continuation order to receive immediately upon publication all new volumes. Should you find that these volumes no longer serve your needs, your order can be cancelled at any time without notice.

The Editors and the Publisher will be glad to receive suggestions or outlines of suitable titles, review or symposia for editorial consideration: if found acceptable, rapid publication is guaranteed.

ROBERT MAXWELL
Publisher Pergamon Press

Linguistic Theory
and Structural Stylistics

by

TALBOT J. TAYLOR

University of Oxford

PERGAMON PRESS

OXFORD • NEW YORK   TORONTO • SYDNEY • PARIS • FRANKFURT

U.K.	Pergamon Press Ltd., Headington Hill Hall, Oxford OX3 OBW, England
U.S.A.	Pergamon Press Inc., Maxwell House, Fairview Park, Elmsford, New York 10523, U.S.A.
CANADA	Pergamon of Canada, Suite 104, 150 Consumers Road, Willowdale, Ontario M2J 1P9, Canada
AUSTRALIA	Pergamon Press (Aust.) Pty. Ltd., P.O. Box 544. Potts Point, N.S.W. 2011, Australia
FRANCE	Pergamon Press SARL, 24 rue des Ecoles, 75240 Paris, Cedex 05, France
FEDERAL REPUBLIC OF GERMANY	Pergamon Press GmbH, 6242 Kronberg-Taunus, Hammerweg 6, Federal Republic of Germany

First edition 1981
British Library Cataloguing in Publication Data
Taylor, Talbot J.
Linguistic theory and structural stylistics.
- (Language and communication library; vol.2)
1. Language and languages - Style
2. Structural linguistics
I. Title   II. Series
149'.9   P301   80-40711

ISBN 0-08-025821-2

PREFACE

In recent years many of the fundamental assumptions of linguistics have been questioned. However, one assumption which continues to hold sway concerns the function of language in communication. According to this view the principal function of language is to enable the communication of meaning between speakers. A corollary to this assumption states that if a speech act has a particular communicational effect—e.g. the hearer 'understands' what the speaker means—the explanation of this achievement lies in the fact that the interactants interpret the utterance according to their shared knowledge of the language. Language 'gives' us what we 'get' in communication.

Stylistics has been profoundly affected by its acceptance of this assumption. First, it has meant that its own object of analysis—i.e. verbal style—has had to be defined as a peripheral aspect of communication, distinct from but dependent upon the principal function: the communication of meaning. Secondly, it has been led to accept that the stylistic aspect of communication is teleologically structured in the same way as the linguistic aspect. That is, if a stylistic effect is felt to be communicated by a text, then this effect must somehow be encoded in the observable structural features of the text.

The aim of this book is to examine some of the theoretical dilemmas to which such a view of style, language, and communication inevitably leads. This inquiry is partly analytical and partly historical. In this sense the study of the development of structural stylistics amounts to the analysis of a Wittgensteinian 'language-game'. The rules under which the game of stylistics is played allow for a good deal of variation. This may be seen in the disparity between successive 'schools' of structural stylistics as well as in the curious freedom which every player/theorist has to alter the use of the game's most crucial concepts. Occasionally, this will give rise to a set of proposals which have the appearance of a completely original game, and a 'new wave' of stylistics is acclaimed.

But there are limits beyond which the language-game of stylistics is not able to venture. These are defined by the dominant notion of the function of language in communication. An exploration of the development and limits of structural stylistics will serve to illuminate the consequences entailed—in linguistics as well as in stylistics—by accepting this notion of communication.

My thanks are due to many for academic, financial, and familial support. First, I would like to thank the series editor, Roy Harris, for his generous and patient supervision during the writing of this book.

I am grateful to George Wolf whose unfortunate interest in the philology of dead languages has not prevented him from being both a scathing critic and a dedicated friend. As my somewhat enigmatic guide to the philosophy of language, he alone is to be blamed for any shortcomings this book may have. For their perceptive comments on earlier drafts of the manuscript I would like to thank Gordon Baker, Roger Fowler, Gill Grebler, John Heritage, Brian McHale, and Michael Toolan. I must make special mention of Jonathan Culler whose criticism and advice over the past few years have been most helpful. Furthermore, I want to acknowledge the inestimable value to me of the guidance and encouragement I have received from two of my friends in Rennes: Suzanne Allaire and Jean Gagnepain.

I am also indebted to Mr. and Mrs. G.R. Furse who have faithfully supported me throughout my studies. I thank them for their generosity and understanding. Finally no amount of thanks would be enough for my parents and for my wife. Without their love and encouragement my work could never have begun. So it is to them that the finished product is dedicated.

T.J. Taylor
Trinity College, Oxford
April 1980

CONTENTS

1

The Concept of Style

A theory of style is a theory of communication. As such stylistics has for the past seventy-five years been under the restrictive sway of a theory of communication imported from linguistics. This situation has provided various benefits for linguistics, including making it possible to define what belongs centrally to language. At the same time, it has led to the founding of a modern theory of style: structural stylistics.

The concept of style, it may be seen, poses a theoretical problem for an autonomous linguistics and so provides a potential source of criticism for any abstract model of language. In general, linguistic theory explains verbal communication in terms of an abstract system linking expression and meaning. The critic of this theory might object that such a system explains very little—if anything—about communication since, when we communicate verbally with another person, there is much more involved than a simple transmission of meanings. One might then ask: what can linguistic theory tell us about these other important aspects of verbal communication? Is its explanation limited to that small part of communication to which we refer when we talk about the meanings of words and sentences? If so, then what is the justification of this restriction? The self-imposed limitation of linguistic theory might be seen as a necessary methodological convenience in order that the continuum of experience may be amenable to scientific analysis. But such a methodological abstraction, required for the purpose of explaining verbal communication in terms of the use of a language, might also be claimed to be misleading or, at best, uninformative. For it simply no longer represents the true nature of communicational phenomena. Such criticisms raise the question of the nature of the relation between language and communication. It is at the nexus of this relation that the concept of style takes its place.

For this reason the practitioners of structural stylistics were led to discuss the function of language in communication. Style was explained as a product of that function. An examination of the structuralist concept of style, therefore, may serve two purposes. It should reveal the fundamental assumptions about communication that are presupposed by linguistic theory. Furthermore, it should clarify the nature and the source of the problems which confront any structural investigation of style.

Since the concept of style is only one of many social science concepts, this chapter will begin by the investigation of the function and nature of social scientific concepts in general. 'How do these concepts arise?' and 'What function do they have?' will be the type of question posed. Then, because the structural concept of style both arose within and was investigated from the perspective of modern linguistics, an examination of the relations between that concept and those of linguistics will follow.

The role of concepts in the social sciences

A characteristic feature of concepts in the social sciences is that in order to be plausible at all they have to be relatable to what the 'man-in-the-street' recognizes as his experience of the world. In most cases, this is not easily accomplished. It is no secret that social scientists themselves do not always agree on the definitions of their terms. As an example, one might take the controversies over the use of such theoretically central terms as 'personality', 'society', 'meaning', 'language', and 'style'. Fortunately, however, the ordinary language-user does not encounter such difficulties. For, in spite of the variety of conflicting definitions, the usefulness of these terms is not thereby impaired.

It is the embarrassing position of stylistics, and indeed of any social science, that no matter how much theorists may disagree about the definitions of such terms as 'style', 'personality', 'market forces', 'civilization', etc., even to the point of questioning the existence of referents for these terms, non-theorists do nonetheless employ such terms in perfectly satisfactory communicational exchanges. Such expressions constitute the lexical staple of our everyday diet of conversation and common-sense theorizing about life, individuals, and communication. As far as the purposes of ordinary communication are concerned, the theoretical debates over the vocabulary of the social sciences do not seem to matter. In contrast to academic discussion, in everyday conversation only the pedant stops to ask 'But what do you mean by "personality"?' or 'How do you mean "style"?'

This is not to say that the scientist wants only to learn just how and when to use certain terms in conversation. His interests lie instead in the (perhaps imaginary) phenomena to which those terms are thought to refer. One does not expect the astronomer, in spite of the name of his profession, to be satisfied with his research when it has advanced to the stage where, without creating confusion among his interlocutors, he can point to the sky and say: 'That's the Milky Way'. Nor should we expect the stylistician or psychologist to be satisfied with a sound knowledge of the everyday usage of the words 'style' and 'personality'.

On the other hand, some social scientists, impressed by the skill reflected in the unproblematic lay usage of such terms, have incorporated into the goals of their theories the aim to account for this linguistic talent of lay members of society. In linguistics, a well-known methodological approach is founded on the premise that if a particular type of verbal response by language-users can be predicted by a linguistic theory, then that theory has a strong claim to empirical validity. What is interesting about this premise, inasmuch as it is adopted by linguistics, is that it reflects a curious theory of language use. That is, it claims that if native speakers agree on speaking of one group of utterances as 'grammatical' and another as 'synonymous', then the characteristic meanings which specialists ascribe to these terms must therefore apply to the utterances themselves. The fact that the use of such terms is itself determined by linguistic and social conventions is not taken into account.

Such a method cannot tell to what extent the informant's response is influenced by his knowledge of the use of the relevant metalinguistic label, e.g. the word 'grammatical'. That is, the informant may, to a certain extent, be responding to his knowledge that sentences such as *That's the motorbike what I saw* are, by virtue of their form, labelled 'ungrammatical'. This may be in spite of the fact that he and his friends regularly use *what* to introduce relative clauses. Here, his disposition to call the test sentence 'ungrammatical' is conditioned by the fact that he has been trained (in school or by his family) to call relative clauses beginning with *what* ungrammatical. Such a response does not then offer an indication of the informant's intuitive sense of grammaticality but only of his disposition to use the words 'grammatical' and 'ungrammatical'. Furthermore, his disposition to use those two words is no more revealing of his linguistic knowledge than is his disposition to use any other pair of words.

Nevertheless, it happens that such an approach will ordinarily suffice. That is to say, there is usually no pressure on an established theory to change if it in fact conforms to the intuitions of the non-specialist members of society. However, if, in the investigation of the empirical grounds of such common-sense intuitions, it appears that what can be observed 'objectively' does not indeed conform to such supposedly 'subjective' intuitions, then this conflict will often serve as a catalyst either to change the accepted views or to force social scientists to search elsewhere for coherent explanations of the observed phenomena.

What the social scientist *does* look for is a greater knowledge of the phenomena whose existence would seem to be implied by the frequent use of ordinary terms such as 'style', 'personality', 'meaning' and so on. But what is problematic about the social sciences is that, in trying to acquire more than the simple knowledge of the usage of certain terms, the investigator finds that there is no 'given' object of investigation. Whereas—by analogy with the reference to 'real things' by natural science terms such as 'head', 'stone', 'star', etc.—the existence of particular phenomena seems to be *implied* by the frequent, unproblematic use of social science terms, there is no easy verification of this implication of existence. One speaks with equal ease and assurance of, say, both rocks and languages. But if precision of reference is required, rocks may be found. Where does one find a language? Can one point to a style?

If, for instance, the methods of the natural sciences were applied to what we conceive of as communicational behaviour, it is possible that certain patterns and regularities in speech could be found. However, nowhere would one discover 'a language', such that the use of that expression would conform in any approximate way to its use today by linguists and laymen alike. The concept of a language, like that of a meaning, is something of a different sort from observable phenomena. This would also apply to the concepts referred to by 'society', 'personality', 'economy', and 'style', and yet these concepts function as objects of social scientific investigations. Our inquiry into the discipline of stylistics may avoid some unnecessary confusion by pursuing a preliminary investigation into the function of one such social object, 'a language', in the elaboration of a social scientific theory.

The social scientist would appear to be under the influence of two antithetical methodological alternatives. He can study the way we talk about behaviour. This amounts to studying the use of certain terms in particular 'language-games'. But this approach will inevitably confuse the user's knowledge of the use of these terms—i.e. knowledge of linguistic and social conventions—with his knowledge of the phenomena to which they are supposed to refer. On the other hand, he can attempt to imitate the methods of the natural sciences and carry out a controlled observation (involving experimentation, statistics, etc.) not of the way we talk about behavior but about behavior itself. Of course it is important not to neglect that this amounts to formulating *more* talk about behaviour, to creating a different language-game relating to behaviour in addition to the one we already have. The important difference of the behaviourist's or observer's language-game is that it implements the use of certain criteria by which our ordinary language-games can permissibly be called 'wrong' or 'misleading'. The scientist's language-game, in this sense, brings in a second opinion by a supposedly impartial judge. But, all the same, an approach attempting to adhere completely to a methodological imitation of the natural sciences could never tell us even as much as what we do already *know*, pre-scientifically, about behaviour, nor how we could have arrived at such knowledge. For we already know that when someone utters certain sounds he is insulting us, or inviting us to a party, or explaining a complex theory of biogenetics. To attempt to explain how we could possibly arrive at such complex knowledge would seem beyond the capabilities of the hypothetically unbiased observer and recorder of behaviour. Yet this knowledge would seem to be an integral feature of that very behaviour.

The dialectical opposition between these two methodological influences on the study of human behaviour demands resolution if only because it appears to be resolved by us all, as non-scientists, every day. For instance, the so-called language-user, in contrast to someone who is not gifted with the faculty of speech, does not merely 'objectively' observe the noises emitted by the person he is facing. Instead he treats those noises as speech and speaks of them as having 'a meaning'; as conforming or not conforming to the laws of 'a language'. Taking noises not as noises, but e.g. as an invitation to a party, is something which we do all the time and yet which requires more of a hearer than objective observation.

Instead, as linguists since Saussure explain, it requires a transformation of the sound-perception by means of an analysis of the sounds *as* an instance of speech. In other words it requires 'seeing' speech not from the perspective of an outsider armed with *explicit* knowledge, but from the perspective of an insider, someone who *implicitly* knows about speech. Not surprisingly, it is in our experience of perceiving sounds from this 'member's' perspective that investigators hope to find the source of our everyday talk about language, languages, meanings, sentences, and so on.

In sum, although the scientific approaches to the study of behaviour may be seen to be divided between the *investigation* of our implicit member's knowledge of behaviour and the *development* of an explicit observer's knowledge of behaviour, this opposition appears to be successfully resolved everyday by members of the human community. Impressed by these successes social scientists have been led to formulate theoretical approaches to the study of human behaviour which reflect such a synthesis. The result is the formulation of social objects.

Just as the natural sciences operate by an abstraction of certain properties and laws from the appearance of the physical world, the social sciences often proceed by the abstraction from the appearance of the social world, i.e. from human behaviour. The result of this abstraction is reflected in the uses of such terms as 'personality', 'society', 'language', 'a language' and 'style'. Of course, the concept, say, of a language refers to different properties of behaviour than does that of personality. Just as the concept of redness involves an abstraction from certain perceived similarities in concrete objects, the concept of a language concerns a point of view from which certain features of behaviour are perceived as the same (i.e. as linguistic). In this way, the expression 'a language' is used to refer to the particular, human way of organizing, analyzing, and interpreting certain features of behaviour. It refers to a hypothetical system with which we perform the transformation of noise into speech. It is in this sense that we speak of this expression—like the other social science expressions listed above—as referring to 'an abstract social object'.

Of course, the sameness attributed to certain features of behaviour—by saying that they are linguistic, or that they manifest social order or personality or intention, etc.—is a sameness or similarity which is, in effect, 'in the eye of the beholder'. For it is only from a particular perspective that two features can be appreciated for certain similarities. In other words, it is a sameness 'in certain respects' which is here in question, and these respects are determined by the perspective taken.

But is there anything which *a priori* determines the perspective to be taken by the social scientist, the perspective from which behaviour may be seen as involving certain patterns of similarities and differences? There certainly seems to be no such obvious choice. Instead, it is not surprising that what guides the choice of perspective from which to approach study of behaviour is the fact that the social scientist is himself a producer and experiencer of human behaviour. As such he already has certain common-sense presuppositions about behaviour, for without these presuppositions he could not participate in all that we qualify as 'human'. The 'behaving' human performs an operation of analysis on experience, thereby transforming, for instance, sounds into speech or behaviour into a manifestation of personality. And we have developed ways of talking about this analysis. The influential forces of (a) the ways in which man interprets and produces behaviour and (b) the ways we have of talking about this interpretation and production are so strong that it should be no surprise that his approach to the description and explanation of behaviour starts from this same dual perspective. There is no doubt that the abstract objects of the social sciences are not constructed 'out of thin air'. Instead they are formulated according to the investigator's identification and interpretation of certain features of behaviour. And the choice of those features can be seen to depend very much on the investigator's experience both in human behaviour and in talking about behaviour. His approach is, in effect, an extension of these experiences. In other words, what the social scientist knows about human behaviour stems as much from these two aspects of his practical knowledge—as a 'behaving' and conversant human—as it does from the observational knowledge of the scientist. The difficulty lies in his efforts to separate and/or to integrate these sources.

Concepts in linguistic theory

Preliminarily, we may recognize that 'style' is used to refer to certain aspects of communicational behaviour. It is generally recognized that for at least the last seventy years the discipline of linguistics has been at the forefront of communication studies. Furthermore, it goes without saying that what is taken to be the 'object of investigation' of linguistics is language. The question arises as to what sort of relation is envisaged between the study of language and the study of communicational behaviour. It will be seen that how this question is treated determines also what is conceived of as being the task of stylistic analysis.

From the point of view of linguistics, the crux of the communicational act is seen to lie in the causal relation between the sounds uttered by a speaker and the meaning that these sounds have for his hearer(s). A more schematic representation of this account may be seen in the following model:

> On an occasion O, A utters U to B who thereby experiences or 'understands' M.

It is presumed that this is a relatively uncontroversial model of linguistic communication because it does not explicitly state how or why the hearer B experiences or understands whatever he does. Instead, this would be an explanatory goal of linguistics.

Modern linguistic theory has approached the study of language carrying some traditional conceptual baggage. There are at least two common-sense assumptions about language to which linguistic theory has responded.

First of all it would seem almost nonsensical to deny the common-sense assumption that we communicate through the use of a language: English, French, Dutch, etc. The corollary to this assumption is that everything (or nearly everything) an English speaker says stands in relation to his language, English, and that because of this he is able to communicate with other people who know English. This assumption makes no precise claims as to what the abstract social object—a language—might be, but claims only that we all speak a language and that it is by virtue of this fact that we are able to communicate. It is the linguist's chosen task to explain how the use of a language is involved in communication acts.

A second common-sense assumption is that a language enables communication because, for all interlocutors, it systematically fixes the relation between expressions and their contents. Furthermore, knowledge of this systematic relation, available to all members of the speech-community, is considered to be the fundamental part of 'knowledge of the language'. This second assumption, it would seem, is what Bloomfield means when he speaks of 'the constancy of meanings' and of 'the specific and stable character of language as a presupposition of language study'.[1] If the relations between expressions and contents were not inter-subjectively given—the argument from this assumption might ask—how could millions of people possibly communicate with each other on billions of different occasions without, in each case, first setting down the rules to guide their communication acts? And what of the generally acknowledged insight of the treatment of a language—like English—in the scores of dictionaries and grammars? The weight of both tradition and common-sense legislate for the acceptance of these two presuppositions of the linguistic view of communication. These assumptions are, first, that it is by the use of a language that we communicate, and second, that a language is a system which fixes, for all its users, the relations between expressions and contents. I will speak of these two common-sense assumptions, concerning the inter-subjective role of languages, as referring to what a language does and what a language is. Together they elaborate the fundamental reductionist principle underlying both linguistics and stylistics, viz. language 'gives' us what we 'get' in communication.

We may better understand the questions raised by these fundamental presuppositions, as well as their relevance to stylistic analysis, if, first, we examine a critical pragmatic difficulty in the analysis of the expression and content planes of verbal communication.

[1]Bloomfield 1935, p. 144.

As is implied by Saussure in his *Cours de linguistique generale*[2] and explicitly stated by Bloomfield in *Language*,[3] no two utterances are ever exactly alike. It is a fundamental discovery of experimental phonetics that what we intuitively might call the 'same' expressions, uttered in the mouths of different speakers or by the same speakers at different times, are never exact duplicates. There is always at least a slight degree of acoustic variation. Furthermore, the relevance of that 'same' expression to the communication situations in which it occurs may be seen to vary with the particular occasion of its utterance. Its communicational content does not remain invariant. As we never seem to live the exact same situations twice it seems reasonable that, at the very least, the particular content (or communicational relevance) of an utterance will never twice be the same. And yet, in spite of this revelation, we still speak of two people on different occasions, uttering the same expression with the same content. But if neither the sounds nor the relevance to communication are ever exactly alike, on what do we base this assumption? How could there possibly exist an invariant relation between expression and content, a relation systematically fixed by the language?

From the point of view of the linguist, although this difficulty may seem disturbing at first sight, its resolution brings to light the usefulness of explaining communication acts in terms of the use of a particular social object, i.e. a language. If a spoken utterance—e.g. one which may be written *This is my breakfast*—may be seen from the dual points of view of expression and content as always, from one situation to the next, differing in *substance* (to use Saussure's term), nevertheless, from the point of view of the English language, it is always one and the same sentence. It has, in Saussure's terminology, the same *form*. In other words, when I say (what the I.P.A. authorizes us to write as) /ais iz maj brekfast/ on July 9th, October 12th, and Christmas Day and when my brother and his young child say these sounds, it will always be possible to find differences between the sounds uttered and between the relevance of those sounds to each of the situations in which they occur. Even so, they are still all supposed to represent instances of the same sentence. Evidence to support this claim may be said to lie in the fact that the sounds which were spoken by me on different dates, by my brother, and by his child are all represented graphically in only one way: *This is my breakfast.*

The claim that all these are instances of the same sentence may be seen to be entailed by what Bloomfield called 'the fundamental assumption of linguistics', namely:

In certain communities (speech-communities) some speech-utterances are alike as to form and meaning.[4]

[2]Saussure 1978, p. 165.
[3]Bloomfield 1935, p. 76.
[4]Bloomfield 1935, p. 144.

The common-sense theoretical weight behind this assumption is considerable. We have already noticed that many strings of speech-sounds are intuitively considered as variants of one invariant form if it is the case that they are written by the same ordered set of graphemes. Further common-sense support lies in the evidence of successful communication between speakers day after day, year after year. If every utterance is conceived of as different from every other, and indeed, every speech-sound from every other, one might wonder how we could ever learn to communicate so successfully amongst ourselves. Every linguistic experience would be unique. But we *do* (at least apparently) communicate successfully, and we do not seem to invent a new set of linguistic conventions every time we speak. It would seem to be an empirical truth that our speech falls into patterns which are repeated both by ourselves and by other people the world over who 'speak our language'. Although it would be difficult to prove beyond all reasonable doubt, the combined evidence of such regularity—reflected in the regular transcription of speech into writing—coupled with the mass of evidence of successful communication and with the patterns of our talk about speech and language seem all to argue convincingly for the acceptance of Bloomfield's 'fundamental linguistic assumption'.

Acceptance of this proposition implies that if every utterance is empirically different in expression-substance from every other, yet some are alike as to linguistic form (that is, expression-form), then, as far as the *linguistic* aspects of communication are concerned, only some differences are relevant. Thus the linguist draws the distinction between what Bloomfield calls the 'linguistic' and the 'non-linguistic' features of speech sound.

The development of this assumption maintains that although every expression is unique, many are the same *in respect to a particular criterion*. This criterion—as it is formulated in the linguistic methodology since Saussure—is meaning. Two expression-substances may display differences, but if their inter-substitution in syntagmatic contexts does not produce a difference in meaning, then their difference is non-linguistic. They are instances of the same linguistic *form*. Thus although the pronunciation by two speakers of what we write as *eat* may differ in the length of the vowel, this difference is not a relevant distinction in English if it creates no difference in meaning. Accordingly, we may understand why the variant pronunciations of *This is my breakfast* may be regarded as tokens of the same formal type.

> As long as we pay no attention to meanings we cannot decide whether two uttered forms are 'the same' or 'different'.[5]

Now, it must be recognized that an essential feature of this distinction between

---

[5]Bloomfield 1935, p. 77.

token substances and formal types is that it relies on a balance of criteria. Formal similarities and differences of expression are determined by the criterion of meaning. In other words, *from the point of view of their meaning,* two expressions are the same even though they are purely acoustically or articulatorily different. But this determination of similarity in respect to a criterion is not as unidirectional as it might appear. For, in order to explain speech in terms of the use of a language, knowledge of which is available to all members of the speech-community, not only must the features of expression-substance be reduced, through application of the criterion of meaning, to those of expression-forms, but also the features of the communicational relevance or content that sounds may have must be reduced to the similarly formal domain of meaning. This notion of a balance of criteria requires further explanation.

We have already established that to call two expressions the same in form involves attributing to them, at the same time, sameness of meaning. (Hence homonyms under the structuralist perspective are often seen as two distinct forms.) But how is sameness of meaning to be established? *For the purpose of delimiting forms,* what is to be counted as meaning and what is to be ruled out? It is obvious that the meaning of an utterance is part of its relevance to communication, but is it all that is relevant? Our common sense tells us that other features of an utterance may also be relevant to a particular communication act: for instance, style, situational register, and dialectal variation of the utterance may be important along with whether the utterance explicitly performs any conventional act, i.e. whether it is a performative. But all these features of the possible communicational relevance or content of an utterance cannot serve as criteria for the delimitation of forms without entailing the rejection of our common-sense notions about 'sameness of form'. For example, *I apologize,* uttered in certain contexts, performs the act of apology. In other contexts it does not (e.g. A: 'What do you do if you have unwittingly insulted a friend.' B: 'I apologize.'). Would we want to say that there are two linguistic forms involved here? (Some linguists would.) If this question seems trivial perhaps the following examples will clarify the dilemma.

When a child rings his father at the office he might say to the secretary who answers the phone *May I speak to Mr. Arbuthnot?* Because of the secretary's familiarity with the voice of the speaker he/she may respond *Of course, Michael; I'll put you through.* Is the communication of the identity of the speaker to be considered part of the meaning of the utterance *May I speak to Mr. Arbuthnot?* In this case certain features of the expression-substance, which are never represented graphically, undoubtedly do have a relevance to the communication involved. That is, they do possess a communicational content in this situation. And yet when his father is at a conference in a distant city and the boy reaches the receptionist to ask *May I speak to Mr. Arbuthnot?*, these expression features do not have the same communicational relevance. Are the two utterances therefore instances of different expression-forms? (It could, of course, be argued that those same features of Michael's voice do have a relevance to the communication with the receptionist but not the same as with Mr. Arbuthnot's secretary. The receptionist might be said to know, by virtue of Michael's voice, that the speaker is not e.g. the conference organizer. But this too would imply that the two utterances involve two different expression-forms.)

Another example: when Michael asks his mother *What time is dinner?* she replies *Don't rush me, dear. You mustn't be so impatient.* Yet when a guest, worried that traffic will make his arrival later than planned, asks Mrs. Arbuthnot *What time is dinner?*, she responds *Oh, some time around 7:30. We'll wait for you.* In the first case the question is taken as another instance of Michael's impatience at dinner time, whereas, in the second case, it is seen as a request for information. Still, we speak of the two utterances as being one and the same sentence, i.e. the same linguistic form, even though in each case the communicational content is different.

Common sense may tell us that in each of the two examples only one sentence is involved. The linguist will confirm that although the communicational content of each utterance may vary from situation to situation and from speaker to speaker, the 'linguistic meaning' remains the same. To include all the communicational content of an utterance as part of its meaning would by some linguists be called a confusion of 'connotation' with 'denotation', by others a confusion of 'situational meaning' with 'linguistic meaning' and by others a confusion of 'non-cognitive meaning' with 'cognitive meaning'. Almost all would agree that some such division must be drawn. Otherwise, formal linguistic analysis would not be possible for we would simply never be able to isolate any invariant properties in speech. This isolation depends, as we have seen, on a criterial perspective, in respect of which sameness of form may be established. But if the total relevance of an utterance is taken as criterion, no sameness would be found. Instead the methodology of linguistic analysis depends on the isolation of a particular domain of communicational content from which sameness of form may be measured. And, as we have seen, in order to preserve our common-sense notion of verbal communication as the use of the particular social object that is a language, we need to retain the notion of some expressions as 'the same' in form. As Bloomfield argued:

Only on this assumption can we account for our ordinary use of language.[6]

This balance of criteria, according to which language is viewed as *sui generis* and on which the methodology of linguistics (and stylistics) depends, may be summarized as follows.

[6]Bloomfield 1935, p. 76.

(a) Only certain features of expression-substance are relevant to the differentiation of content-forms (i.e. meanings). These features serve to delimit expression-forms.

(b) Only certain aspects of content-substance (i.e. communicational relevance) are relevant to the differentiation of expression-forms. These aspects serve to delimit content-forms or meanings.

The analytical balance is one of perspective. The distinction of expression-substance from expression-form is made according to the criterion of relevance to content-form. In mirror fashion, the separation of content-form from content-substance is made from the criterial perspective of expression-form. Each plane is analysed into form and substance by reference to the formal dimension of the other plane. By this dual reduction of their investigatory domain, linguists are able to formulate a theoretical concept of what a language is that accords with our common-sense notion of what a language is for, that is, to use for the communication of inter-subjective meanings. On such reductionist foundations the linguist builds his explanation of how language 'gives' us what we 'get' in communication.

We have seen that in order to establish criteria for the determination of formal identity of expression, linguistics is forced to consider as relevant only certain features of the possible communicational content of speech. A possible question here might be: by what criteria are these features of communicational content the same? It would of course be simple but circular to claim that they are the same in respect of their role as criteria for the delimitation of forms. Do we take the two utterances of *May I speak to Mr. Arbuthnot?* as same in meaning in order that we may establish if they are instances of the same expression-form? Or do we take it as given that they are instances of the same expression-form in order to discover if they are the same in meaning? Either way would be begging a crucial question relating to the primary dilemma of linguistic analysis: where to begin? Instead, if the linguist is to avoid being trapped in this theoretical circle—a trap which seems to raise no problem for the ordinary speaker/hearer—he must choose a *ground*: i.e. some method, outside of this criterial balance, by which he can determine linguistic meaning.

In his book *Synonymy and Linguistic Analysis,* Roy Harris points out the crucial role that the attribution of sameness of meaning—what he calls 'synonymity statements'—plays in the analysis of linguistic forms. The orthodox analysis of the expression-plane of language requires that sameness or difference of meaning be determinable. But, in the final chapter, he argues,

> It would be idle to discuss the role of synonymity statements in grammar and semantics unless it could be shown that, in principle, it is feasible to formulate procedures which will make the construction of synonymity statements

for L possible. But procedures of this kind cannot be formulated independently of the adoption of some specific concept of 'linguistic knowledge'; for we cannot ultimately say what will count as evidence for or against a given synonymity statement unless we are clear about where the boundary between the linguistic and the non-linguistic lies.[7]

There are of course many philosophical theories of meaning which seek to isolate the phenomena of linguistic meaning within the wider range of communicational or interactional relevance. Many of these are implicitly (i.e. dictionaries) or explicitly based on the criteria of truth-conditions and extension. According to this approach, the use of words to refer to objects is seen as the fundamental basis of meaning from which all other varieties of meaning are derived. These theories will not be dealt with here as they are not, in general, used to ground the practical application of a linguistic method based on the model of the inter-determination of form and meaning. Instead linguists find the ground of this balanced view of language in their common-sense practice of linguistic analysis. There is found to be no need to refer to philosophical theories of semantics.

It is an implicit corollary of Bloomfield's 'fundamental assumption of linguistics' that writing is a faithful transcription of speech *salva significatione.* No one expects writing to capture the effects of intonation, or voice, or tone, or of various situational variables, but one does expect the transcription of a speech utterance into writing to 'mean the same'.[8] In this way, if native English speakers are inclined to say, no matter what the particular features of context, voice, intonation, etc. that *This is my breakfast* means the same as a string of sounds uttered by a particular individual at a particular time, then everything points toward the logic of taking them as instances of the same linguistic form, i.e. of the same sentence. It is this common-sense notion which provides a ground to the balance of criterial perspective on which linguistic analysis depends. By appealing to such intuitions, the content 'core' of an utterance is—as far as the demands of practical analysis are concerned—successfully isolated. And, by the use of this core, that is 'linguistic meaning', linguists are provided with a criterion for the differentiation of invariant linguistic form from the variables of expression-substance. Accordingly, the notion of a language may be treated as a question not of disparate noises which could have an infinite range of possible relevances to human behaviour, but of forms which interrelate according to specific criteria to make up an, albeit complex, structure: the social object we call 'a language'. But the strategies employed by the linguist in order to provide himself with such a *sui generis* object of investigation do not have to be seen as gratuitous or artificial. Instead they reflect his efforts to see speech as we all see it in our practical accomplishment of everyday life. He goes to these efforts in

[7]Harris, 1973, p. 146.
[8]For a critical analysis of the 'scriptist' bias in linguistics, see Harris, 1980, pps. 6-18 and 130-2.

order to analyse how it comes about that we see a string of sounds not as such, but as a particular sentence to which the language attaches a particular meaning. The linguist tries to reproduce analytically our everyday 'competence' in dealing with speech. Hence it is not surprising that the ground for the linguist's analytical structure of forms and meanings should consist in a reference to the common-sense notion of 'means the same'. It is an understandably *practical* solution to a theoretical analysis of *practical* behaviour.

It is important, however, to recognize the consequences of the integration of theory and practicality in this approach. Before considering the consequences for the field of stylistics, a look at the consequences for general linguistics may be illuminating. Consider the following examples discussed by Jacques Bonnet and Joel Barreau in their *L'Esprit des mots:*[9]

(1) *la ville de Rome* - The city of Rome.
(2) *les remparts de Rome* - The walls of Rome.

Although we intuitively sense a difference in the relations holding between *Rome* and *ville* in (1) from those holding between *Rome* and *remparts* in (2), there are, on the face of it, no purely formal distinctions to account for this; i.e. in both cases the words are linked by *de* and word order is the same. Traditional grammar would say that in (1) *Rome* is in apposition to *ville*, whereas in (2) *Rome* is the complement of the noun *remparts*. Such an analysis does reflect that there is a communicationally relevant distinction to be drawn between the relations exemplified in (1) or (2) even though it is not reflected in the formal organization of the graphic substance—i.e. the written sentences themselves.

Such a situation presents the linguist with two choices. Either he says that the communicationally relevant distinction is not part of the linguistic meaning of the two utterances and thus explains the similarity of form, or he says it *is* part of the meaning. If the latter choice is taken, the linguist is faced with explaining why the formal structures of the sentences do not seem to reflect this difference. Some might claim that this is a case of grammatical homonymy, on the analogy of lexical homonymy. An explanation of the difference in meaning which is related to the claim of grammatical homonymy is one which has recently become much more popular in linguistics; this is to postulate the existence of a hidden layer of form which, in the case of (1) and (2), would not be the same. Thus transformational-generative grammar would claim that although their 'surface' structures do not account for the difference in meaning between (1) and (2), it may however be accounted for by the different 'deep' structures underlying the surface sentences. Again the presupposition is evident in such linguistic reasoning that that which counts as a form is determined by the criterion of meaning.

[9]Bonnet and Barreau 1974, p. 19.

Whether or not one perceives a difference in meaning here will determine whether a difference of form is also to be postulated; if two meanings are detected, two forms must be the cause. The reverse case may be seen in the earlier transformational explanation of grammatical relations holding between actives and passives. On the assumption, based on an appeal to common-sense, that active and passive sentences have the same meaning, it is argued that they must therefore have the same underlying form even though their surface structures are so different. Hence *Caesar conquered Gaul* and *Gaul was conquered by Caesar* are said to have the same 'underlying' form. Same meaning implies same form; different meaning, different form. Thus those who approach grammar in this way are able to claim that their method has more 'power' since it is able to explain such differences and similarities in meaning without having to recur to the confusing notions of grammatical homonymy and ambiguity. Their method does not require such a retreat from the fundamental criterial balance of the two planes of expression and content.

But unfortunately, this approach has consequences which are reflected in the current disarray, and disagreement between, various linguistic 'schools'. For all depends in this, or in any such 'biplanar' approach, on what is to be counted as meaning and what is to be ruled out. One linguist may claim that the use of an active rather than a passive can have a relevant effect on communication. If he sees this effect as part of linguistic meaning then he has support for the claim that actives and passives are not generated from the same underlying form. If another says such a difference is 'only an optional factor of style' he thereby has evidence to support the claim of identical 'deep' or underlying structures. If both are native speakers, who is to decide between them? And how? It all depends on what one counts as 'meaning' for the purposes of constructing synonymity statements, i.e. of determining whether two utterances are 'the same' or 'different'. It is to this, unfortunately, that the application and development of Bloomfield's 'fundamental assumption of linguistics' leads.

Such an approach to the determination of meaning and form is the practical foundation of modern linguistic analysis. It is on the basis of this approach that linguistics has been able to advance as far as it has. But it has produced certain consequences outside of the realm of 'linguistics proper'. The development of modern stylistics is one.

The concept of style within the linguistic perspective

The isolation, for the purposes of linguistic analysis, of a particular aspect of communicational content as 'linguistic meaning' has facilitated the explanation of at least a part of the act of communication seen in terms of the use of a language. The latter, under this explanation, is conceived of as *sui generis*, i.e. as a conventionalized system of relations between expression-forms and content-forms (meanings). However, although this explanatory approach may provide a practical method for the analysis of the nature and function of the common-sense notion of 'a language', it leaves unexplained a whole variety of aspects of the communicational relevance of speech. In a sense, linguists have carved out of the phenomena of the expression and content of communicational behaviour those aspects which they see as belonging to them. After all, they say, the object of linguistic investigation *is language*. Consequently, linguists analyse those aspects of communication which they see as belonging to their province of explanation, and have left the rest to scholars of other disciplines to analyse. And it is by virtue of this balanced inter-determination of expression-form and meaning, i.e. by virtue of the development from Saussure's *Cours de linguistique generale*, that linguists claim to escape any criticism to the effect that they have left so much of verbal communication unexplained.

Furthermore, the linguist's model that is derived from Saussure's pioneering notion of 'langue' and from Bloomfield's 'fundamental assumption'—that is, the bi-planar model based on the inter-determination of expression-form and meaning—is so firmly rooted in common-sense that it almost seems nonsensical to question it. For, if the sceptic does not accept the reduction of the pertinent aspects of communication to those of linguistic meaning, then the explanation of speech in terms of formal similarity would seem impossible. The conceptual field which organizes our talk about speech in terms of sentences, words, vowels, consonants, prepositions, nouns, verbs, etc. would become groundless. And if one does not assume that there is some formal and semantic constancy in our speech habits, then the notion of verbal communication as involving the use of a language becomes incoherent. But to reject *this* pillar of common-sense is to deny that English speakers use the English language when they speak, and Swahili speakers the Swahili language. This would seem to push scepticism beyond the bounds of common-sense.

The discipline of structural stylistics, as it appears in the writings of Charles Bally, Michael Riffaterre, Roman Jakobson (who referred to the discipline as 'poetics') and the generative stylisticians, arose in order to explain certain common-sense intuitions about verbal communication that are not explicable—at least not at face value—*within* the *sui generis* linguistic model. But the stylistics to which these analysts contributed did not propose to reject or even alter the basic linguistic model as it is outlined above. Instead, this model is quite evidently taken for granted. All of these stylisticians had considerable training in linguistics (although Riffaterre and Jakobson were originally formed in literary studies), and the basic bi-planar model, as inherited from Saussure, plays a central, determining role in their efforts to develop a structural stylistic methodology. The notion that language is both the source and explanation of verbal communication remains paramount. Hence, a search for an explanation of communicational effects other than meaning—e.g. style—inevitably involves an analysis of language, but an analysis from a different point of view. Whereas linguistics analyses how a language is able to be used to produce meaning, stylistics analyses how a language may be used to produce stylistic effects. The notion of 'what a language is' remains the same, but the analysis of what a language can do proceeds from a different perspective entirely. For one the explanatory goal is language's meaning-function, for the other it is the stylistic function.

The use of the expression 'style', concerning the way in which a speaker or writer 'expresses himself', had been commonplace for a long time before the creation of the discipline of stylistics. But, as with many other social scientific concepts, there had been—and remains—no consensus as to just which phenomena are referred to by this term. Nor was there any possible method by which two interlocutors might verify that they were talking about the same thing. This is still the case today, but the rise of modern linguistics has at least narrowed down the range of possible real or hypothetical referents by distinguishing style from the contrary phenomenon of linguistic meaning.

The difficulty of delimiting the social object *style* may be seen to be due to a great extent to the absence of a criterion in respect of which those features of communicational behaviour which we wish to call 'style' could be found to be the same. We have, in fact, no criterion for defining what style is, or for defining what gives rise to stylistic effects. Instead, linguistic stylistics as practised in the 20th century, has only two relatively small footholds from which to proceed: (1) style is not linguistic meaning, and (2) the causal source for stylistic effects must inevitably lie in the structural organization of language. The parallels here with two of the common-sense presuppositions of linguistics—that what a language does is communicate meanings and that it does this due to its particular structural organization—are not coincidental. Linguistics, however, was able to accommodate these two fundamental presuppositions within an overall theory of language based on the inter-determination of expression-form and meaning.

A suitable parallel might be envisaged for the purposes of stylistic analysis. But while linguistics receives intuitive support or grounding in the common-sense notion of 'means the same as', stylistics can find no such common-sense concept on which to ground the practicality of its analysis. Furthermore the stability of the linguistic model is reinforced by our beliefs about languages as social objects (English, French, Dutch, etc.), about the practical adequacy of interlingual translation, about the usefulness of dictionaries and grammars, and about the conversation of meaning in the transcription of speech to written form. These common, everyday intuitions constitute the limits in our Wittgensteinian 'language-game' about verbal communication, and, as such, form the anchors tying the bi-planar linguistic model to our self-projected image of behaviour.

The notion of style is not so secure. 'X is in the same style as Y' is a difficult assertion on which to form an agreement. All will come down to 'But what do you mean by style?' And the notion of a speaker's or writer's style can involve, according to the whims of those debating the definition, a wide variety of further notions from psychology, sociology, literary criticism, linguistics, and other language-games concerning human behaviour. But the notion of whether 'X means the same as Y' always has both the common-sense arbiters of the dictionary and the conditions for true assertion. The justice handed down by these arbiters is by no means unbiased; but in our language-games concerning 'meaning' it has the right to the final word. Such is the firmness of the place occupied by these arbiters in our talk about meaning that further argument only stretches the bounds of common-sense.

As a result, the scientific approach to style, as compared to the scientific approach to language and meaning, must begin without the advantage of a secure foothold in common-sense. Evidence of a recognition of this disadvantage may be seen to lie in habitual efforts of stylisticians to define the object of their investigations before they begin to investigate. Linguists, on the other hand, can count on a certain consensus of opinion about what 'a language' is and what 'meaning' is. Indeed one does often find definitions of these terms in linguistics treatises, but these are generally only adding a precision of reference to the common core of the usage of the terms. Stylisticians, however, have no such common-sense ground on which to construct their object of investigation. Our unproblematic use of 'style' dissolves when efforts towards precision of reference are introduced. So, to the critic who is predisposed to object, the definitions, that are produced will seem arbitrary, as will the methods proposed to investigate 'style' as defined. The circularity inherent in stylistics stems not from any defect in the observed phenomena but from the heterogeneity and imprecision of reference by which the common-sense use of the term 'style' is characterized. The place of the expressions 'a language' and 'meaning' are much more securely fixed in our language-games concerning communication than is that of 'style'. It is no fault of the stylistician if it is always possible to object to his theory with some such statement as: 'Of course it's a perfectly adequate theory for the investigation of certain phenomena. But is that style?'

It is therefore not surprising that each structural stylistician might seem to be investigating a different theoretical object. This is perhaps unavoidable. However, the interest of the work carried out by these men lies in their efforts, in spite of the inherent difficulties, to formulate a scientific method of analysis. Furthermore, their approaches to this task may be seen to exhibit similar presuppositions about the nature of language and of communication, and about the proper form of an investigation into their relations. Since no criterion immediately presents itself by which stylistic features of language-use may be distinguished from other features of communicational relevance, structural stylisticians have endeavoured to set up such a criterion by means of a prior analysis of the function of language in communication. In this they extended the traditional linguistic investigation of what language does beyond the 'secure' realm of the transmission of linguistic meaning. From a general notion of the function of language in communication, they deduce the criteria by which there may be distinguished a particular stylistic (or for Jakobson, 'poetic') function of language. Furthermore, as they all take as 'given' the bi-planar model of language, it is also not surprising that the methods they propose for the analysis of style in language are essentially those of linguistic analysis. In this way, in spite of the lack of a common-sense ground for their notion of style, they all carry out the pioneer investigation of style by means of a methodological development extended out from the security of linguistic explanation. Consequently, their conclusions acquire a certain degree of the common-sense respectability attributed to linguistic analysis proper. They attempt to situate the notion of style within the more general notion of the communicational function of language, and propose to investigate style by extension from the analytical methods of linguistics. As a result structural stylistics has developed a new theme in the social scientific investigation of human behaviour by attempting to extend the explanatory power of the Saussurian bi-planar model of language beyond its chosen domain of investigation to hitherto unexplained aspects of communication. What matters here is not whether these investigators' efforts to reconcile 'language' with 'communication' arrive at the same conclusions, but the reasoning and presuppositions on which these investigations are based.

2

Bally and the Saussurian Origins of Structural Stylistics

Modern stylistics was inaugurated by Charles Bally in his *Traite de stylistique francaise*. Significantly Bally was also one of the first disciples of Ferdinand de Saussure and the editor (along with A. Sechehaye) of Saussure's *Cours de linguistique generale*. Much of what we know of Saussure's pioneering thought in linguistics is seen through the interpretation that these two students made of his teaching.

It is important that Bally's work be seen in the context of the development of Saussurian thought. In this light Bally's work in stylistics may be recognized as an attempt to explain aspects of verbal communication *other* than those accounted for by Saussure's bi-planar model of linguistics. The need for this is clear. Saussure's new model, as it stood, was open to the criticism that its coherence is achieved only by the systematic exclusion of important aspects of communication as irrelevant to the interests of linguistics. Should these aspects have been included within linguistics, it might have been claimed, Saussure's formalistic goals for an autonomous linguistics would have been unattainable. By limiting the extension of the phenomena that were relevant to linguistics, that is, by arbitrarily carving out of the centre of verbal behaviour a domain that was defined *a priori* as uniquely and exclusively linguistic, Saussurian linguistics was vulnerable to the following claim: this all important isolation of the linguistic domain is dictated by methodological requirements rather than by correspondence to the nature of the phenomenon described. But if those excluded, non-linguistic aspects of communication could be provided with a similar explanation, based on the same model and same principles, the force of this claim would be weakened. Ever since, as far as linguistics is concerned, stylistics has had this important but surprisingly unacknowledged role as a buffer zone for the defence of the autonomy of the linguistic domain.

Consequently, the central question asked by Bally's stylistics is: how do communicators link particular features of the expression-plane with content other than meaning? Bally's answer to this question constitutes the first structural explanation of stylistic phenomena. There are four fundamental principles underlying Bally's theory of style.

1.   The structure of a language[1] is teleologically related to requirements im-

---

[1] The problems raised by the translation of the *Cours de linguistique generale* have shown that it is difficult to render into English the distinction therein made between *la langue* and *le langage*. Further-

posed on it by communication. A language is a tool which obeys certain structural laws and yet which adapts itself to the requirements of the task for which it is used. Like linguistics, stylistics concerns itself with how a language makes possible the communication of thought.

2. Thought has two aspects: the conceptual and the non-conceptual. The former is a result of convention while the latter has its source in personal experience and emotion. That is, thought is a product both of objective, conventionally determined concepts and of subjective and private feelings, attitudes, motives, perspectives, etc.

3. Since a language both adapts itself to and makes possible the communication of thought and since thought consists of two aspects, then there must be something about the structure of a language which is the source of the communication of non-conceptual thought. Linguistics focuses on the source of the conceptual function in language. Stylistics, then, should take as its subject matter the source of the affective function in language. That is, stylistics should seek to explain how a language adapts to, and makes possible the communication of, the subjective, non-conceptual aspects of thought.

4. The bi-planar model in linguistics delimits expression-forms by taking the perspective of meaning-differentiation. So, an adequate model of stylistics should discover the structural source of non-conceptual communication by examining the relations between elements of the language from the point of view of their potential for communicating non-conceptual aspects of thought. Different elements of the language would be seen to correlate with different non-conceptual (or what Bally called 'affective') values. This fourth principle, according to which the bi-planar model of linguistics is adopted for use in stylistics, will prove to be characteristic of structural stylistic theory as a whole.

The functional perspective, reflected in these principles, appears to have arisen out of the profound rejection by Saussure and Bally of the historical perspective in linguistics. Bally seems to have considered the abandonment of historical explanation just as important to stylistics as to linguistics. Much of the *Traite de stylistique francaise* is devoted to the advocacy of this view. An explanation of a particular aspect of a language solely in terms of certain facts about the historical evolution of languages was for Bally, as for Saussure, devoid of value. Instead, for Bally at least, knowledge of the use to which language is put in communicational interaction should play a primary role in explaining the structure

---

more, Bally does not always appear rigorously to observe this distinction. For the purposes of this analysis the following usage will be observed: when what is referred to is either *une langue,* in the sense of English, French, Dutch, etc., or *la langue,* in the specific sense fixed by Saussure of a holistic system of conventions governing speech, the expression used here will be 'a (or the) language' (with the exception of those contexts where the untranslated French term seems most adequate). On the other hand, 'language' will be used to refer to linguistic phenomena in general, regardless of any systemic, social, or theoretical perspective.

of that language. For it is due to the demands that communication makes on a language that the language is as it is. Consequently, any method of investigation which ignores this fact would be necessarily incomplete. The following exposition of the reasoning underlying Bally's stylistics will be structured so as to reflect the importance which he attached to this functional perspective.

The dialectic of verbal interaction

For Bally, communicative interaction is a conflict (*lutte*) between the dialectically opposed poles of the speaker's impulse towards personal expression and the restrictive conventions imposed by the requirements of inter-personal communication. Interestingly, this conflict was even seen to affect the very nature of thought by creating the distinction between the affective and the conceptual aspects of thinking. To understand how this is possible we must first examine the more fundamental notion of the dialectic of verbal interaction.

In an article written in 1925 entitled 'Mécanisme de L'expressivité linguistique', he speaks of the antimony between expression, which is individual and affective (pertaining to the emotions, i.e. 'subjective'), and communication, which is inter-personal and analytical, striving to render the messages more objective.

> Thought tends towards personal, affective, integral expression; *la langue* towards the clear and effective communication of thought. Therefore *la langue* can only render the most general traits of thought by depersonalizing and objectifying it.[2]

These two poles of interaction are presented as ever-present yet contradictory. They are never in total harmony with each other. The successful speech act might attain an equilibrium adequate to the needs of a particular interaction, but never is one aspect so dominant that the other will disappear entirely. This state of affairs is not specifically linguistic but is a general, inescapable social fact. Man's ego will always be in conflict with his desire and need to live and interact with other men. Interaction is a form of mediation between the personal and the social.[3]

Bally points out that we habitually speak of man as 'a social animal' and of language as the product of man's social instinct.[4] But, argues Bally, man's individual instincts are far from being subordinated to this social instinct. Instead they strive against his social instinct even though this is inevitably a battle which neither side can ever win. Man's dual tendencies towards individuality and toward socialization remain in perpetual conflict. Nowhere is this conflict more apparent than in his interaction with other individuals.

[2]Bally 1952, p. 82. (All translations from Bally's work are my own.)
[3]See the work of J. Gagnepain for a much more comprehensive exposition of the social dialectic: e.g. *Le Pouvoir Dire* (forthcoming).
[4]Bally 1952, p. 20.

As soon as two people come into contact, the conflict begins. This is because neither an absolute accord nor a perfect harmony between minds is ever possible. but conflict, as I have defined it, is not incompatible with solidarity and mutual sympathy. It simply presupposes an incompatible concordance between beliefs, desires, and wills. The dialectic of interaction, in fact, results from a conflict between the ego of the subject and his social instinct.[5]

Using a language, the nearer the speaker keeps to the norms of the socially conventional forms of expression the greater are his chances of being understood. But since the set of these forms is relatively limited and their conventions of an inherently impersonal nature, the realm of possibilities for personal expression is thus severely restricted.

> Does the language that an individual has inherited from his environment permit him, in each circumstance, to say *all* that he would like to say, and say it how he would like to?...Obviously not.[6]

Still, the further he strays from these conventional norms, in an effort to communicate more personally his thoughts, the greater the realm of possibilities of expression; but, at the same time, he will be stretching the limits of the communicable and endangering the success of the speech act.

Furthermore, Bally argues, perhaps paradoxically, that a language, because of its function as a 'tool' for communication, itself mirrors both aspects of the interactional dialectic. So, a language, although essentially a social and conventional phenomenon, is able to accommodate to a certain degree the personal expressive impulse.

> Is a language therefore unable, of its own accord, to express emotions, desires, and the will? We know quite well that it can.[7]

Primarily, the discipline of stylistics is pictured by Bally as the study of the effect of the force of personal expression on languages. Because of the ever-present impulse towards personal expression in communication, languages themselves are structured in such a way as to allow expressivity. Stylistics, according to Bally, should be the study of the methods of personal expression that a language makes available to its speakers.

> Stylistics studies the elements of a language organized from the point of view of their affective content; that is, the expression of emotions by language as well as the effect of language on the emotions.[8]

[5]Bally 1952, p. 20.
[6]Bally 1952, p. 76.
[7]Bally 1952, p. 82.
[8]Bally 1909, p. 16.

The communication of thought by language

In order to explain Bally's notion of expressivity in language we will have to examine his view of the function of language in interaction: that is, to communicate thought. Secondly, because his work presents an idiosyncratic notion
of thought as well as of how thought is communicated, it may best serve the purposes of this exposition to compare Bally's point of view with that of the surrogational theory of language.[9]

> ...language is made to express what we think.[10]

> But what should be understood by this vague term "thought"? Just what do
> we express by words?[11]

The surrogational theory of language claims that words stand for objects or for
the thoughts representing those objects. The term 'thoughts' is often replaced by
'concepts' or 'ideas' but the sense remains approximately the same. This is a very
simplified account of an influential linguistic theory which is apparent in many
guises from classical times to the present. An explicit version is adopted by John
Locke in book III of his *Essay Concerning Human Understanding*.

> Man, though he have great variety of thoughts, and such from which others
> as well as himself might receive profit and delight; yet they are all within his
> own breast, invisible and hidden from others, nor can of themselves be made
> to appear. The comfort and advantage of society not being to be had without
> communication of thoughts, it was necessary that man should find out some
> external sensible signs, whereof those invisible ideas, which his thoughts are
> made up of, might be made known to others.... The use, then, of words, is
> to be sensible marks of ideas; and the ideas they stand for are their proper
> and immediate signification.[13]

The difference between this theory of language and that advocated by Bally lies
both in contrasting notions of thought and of how thoughts are communicated.
For the surrogationalist such as Locke, words stand for concepts or ideas. Bally
claims that such a theory reduces the notion of intelligence, and of its thoughts,
to that of logic and *idees pures*. He argues that because thought is greatly affected
by experience (even, the *result* of experience: he is not clear on this) and also 'of
service' to our actions, then to imagine it as consisting of logical concepts *alone* is
to misinterpret both its nature and its function.

[9]for an analysis of the genesis of the surrogational theory of language see R. Harris, *The Language-
Makers* (1980).
[10]Bally 1909, p. 4.
[11]Bally 1909, p. 5.
[12]Locke 1961, III, ii, 1.

> Those of my thoughts which arise in the context of everyday life are never essentially intellectual. They are movements accompanied by emotion; pushing me towards action or restraining me from it...Without a doubt, it is by the intellect that I become conscious of these movements; but intellect does not form their essence.[13]

Essentially, Bally pictures thought as something too subjective, too private, too involved in the myriad of ways in which man, as an individual, asserts himself in the world, to be of the order of something so apparently objective, logical, and even conventional as the concept. The role of subjectivity, individuality, and emotion in the formulation of thought, argues Bally, should not be neglected if we are to avoid representing thought as a mere reflected image of the outside world. Instead, thoughts are to be characterized as more or less conceptual (and objective), more or less affective (and subjective). Here again, Bally's notion of the dialectic of interaction illuminates his theory of communication. That is, not only does this dialectic—between the subjective and the objective—regulate the communication of one's thoughts to another; its influence even extends into the composition of thought. For this reason, thought is divided between the poles of the affective and the conceptual.

To a stylistician of the 1980s, Bally's theory may sound charged with its own subjectivity and impressionism and seem quite far removed from the analytical rigours of description and science. This perhaps mistaken view is mainly caused by the disfavour into which has fallen Bally's view of the mind. Contemporary stylistics, and linguistics, however, are no less psychologically based. Whereas Bally's descriptions of thought and communication were couched in a terminology whose only foundation lay in intuition and everyday usage, today theories of thought and communication are veiled in the terms of computational systems, information packages, and programming strategies. Indeed, those modern theorists who argue that the support for a computer model lies in its explanatory power—independently of whether the model is given a realist or nonrealist interpretation—unwittingly provide an argument for the modern-day appreciator of Bally. For, under such an account of the function of theories, it remains to be seen whether the impressionism of Bally's theory of communication and style is a hinderance or a help to its explanatory power. Curiously, Bally seems to have anticipated the mechanist claims of his distant successors and already to have prepared a reply:

> From this perspective, how will language appear to us? It will not appear as an accumulation of words strung into sentences, ordered by mechanical rules, but as a collection of natural phenomena, explained by psychological and social laws.[14]

[13]Bally 1952, p. 15-16.
[14]Bally 1909, p. 5.

To reiterate: like the surrogationalist, Bally does indeed picture the function of language as the communication of thought. But for Bally, the conceptual nature of thought is only one of its two equally important characteristics. Thoughts are partly intellectual (i.e. conceptual), partly affective (i.e. relating to sentiments, personal and social alike). They may therefore be seen as a fusion of objective and subjective characteristics, that is, of that which provokes thought (the objective world) and that which formulates thought (the subjective act of thinking). The other functions of language—e.g. the expression of feelings, the acknowledgement of social status, the imposition of one's opinion, etc.—are supposedly modulated through this primary, essential function of the communication of thought. In other words, for anything in the communication situation to have a linguistic function, it has to be realized inter-subjectively in the thoughts of the speaker and hearer, whether this be a conscious or unconscious realization. In this way, although thought plays an important role in Bally's theory of communication, this theory may be seen to be significantly different from that of the strict surrogationalist.

It should not be inferred that Bally denies that an important function of language is to communicate ideas. Ideas (or concepts) are, for Bally, the product of a 'a judgement by the intellect', as opposed to sentiments, the product of a 'value judgement'. In this way, while sentiments concern the subjective aspect of thought, ideas reflect the thought's effort to be as objective as possible. Ideas are seen as the result of thought's tendency to conform as much as possible to objective reality.[15] They represent the ego's efforts to transcend itself."

It is interesting to note that Bally's notion of 'objective reality'—to which, in the formation of ideas, thought attempts to conform—is a question of social convention. Bally says that because the *signifie* (concept) itself is arbitrary[16], the particular characteristics of the concept evoked by a *signifiant* are a result of the social conventions of the language. A language, therefore, gives structure and shape to the conceptual plane. Bally points out that although we assume that our notion of the colour *green* is derived solely from our experience of perception, it is in fact imposed upon us by the language with which we communicate. The language creates, by convention, the conceptual category of *green* by opposing it to *yellow, blue, red,* etc. This argument is a corollary of the Saussurian opposition (developed further by Hjelmslev in his *Prolegomena to a Theory of Language*) between form and substance. Just as we categorize, in the expression plane, sound-substances into sound-forms according to the criterion of meaning-differentiation, we also categorize, in the content plane, unstructured content-substance into content-forms according to the criterion of formal-differentiation; that is according to the set of sound-forms provided by the language. The colour-spectrum is divided up conceptually (into our concepts of *green, blue,* etc.) in the

[15]Bally 1909, p. 6.
[16]Bally 1952, p. 123.

same way that our language divides it up by providing only a certain limited set of expressions ('green', 'blue', etc.) with which to speak of colour. Accordingly, the form of the conceptual content of an expression—i.e. Bally's 'idea'—is seen as imposed by the conventional structure of the language and not by the nature of the thing to which the expression may refer.

For Bally, arbitrariness, conventionality, and objectivity are all compatible characteristics of the concept. In this sense, the objectivity of a thought is really a question of inter-subjectivity. The objective idea conforms to the social conventionality of the expression of thought by language. Concepts are objective because they are given by the language, the gauge of identity and delimitation which all members of the linguistic community share. Conceptual thought differs from affective thought in that it has its source in social convention rather than in personal impulse. Here it is clear how the international dialectic informs Bally's theory of the communication of thought.

It should be noted that Bally does not picture any thoughts, or the words expressing them, as either purely conceptual or purely affective. Instead, it is seen as a question of being more one or more the other, never total exclusion of one in favour of the other. So, although this is not always readily apparent to the observer, no thought or expression, no matter how conceptual, is ever entirely devoid of affective characteristics, and vice-versa. Instead, Bally speaks of a greater tendency towards the conceptual or towards the affective and, in this way, of an 'intellectual dominant' and of an 'affective dominant'.[17]

> Thought oscillates between perception and emotion...But from the perspective of practical observation, it can be concluded that either intelligence or sentiment is predominant. Thought is oriented towards one or the other of these poles, without ever attaining them. Thoughts have, in each case, either an intellectual dominant or an affective dominant. But thought...demands that language be its reflection....Whether language always succeeds in perfectly realizing this goal, we have no way of knowing. But, in practice, it is certain that language reflects the same dominants that are observable in the life of the mind.[18]

Stylistics, for Bally, is the study of those verbal expressions with an affective dominant. Still for the purposes of our exposition of Bally's method of stylistic analysis, it is important to note that every expression, even the most affective, is supposed to have at least a minimum of intellectual characteristics. Otherwise the expression would not be conventional and hence not part of *la langue*. It is in contrast with its intellectual characteristics that an expression's affective dominant is to be perceived.

[17]Bally 1909, p. 151.
[18]Bally 1909, pp. 151-2.

We have seen that a difference between the surrogational theory of language and Bally's theory lies in their conceptions of thought. Still, not only do both theories see the nature of thought from different perspectives, but their views of how thought is communicated also differ significantly.

For the surrogationalist, words are the names of thoughts, or through thoughts, of that which is represented in thought. Bally argues that thought is communicated in other ways besides naming. The difference between more conceptual and more affective thoughts is reflected in the way in which they are communicated. The more conceptual (or intellectual) a thought is the more directly it can be communicated by means of the language-given, and hence arbitrary, relation between expression and meaning, *signifiant* and *signifié*. This relation is central to the Saussurian theory of language. However, Bally claims that the more 'expressive' (or 'affective': except in restricted contexts, these terms are interchangeable) aspects of thought are *not* communicated directly by the arbitrary relation of *signifiant* to *signifié*. In other words, different aspects of the same thought are communicated by different methods.

In his 1925 article, 'Mecanismé de l'expressivité', Bally argues that the affective aspects of thoughts are communicated by a *jeu d'associations implicites:* an interplay of implicit associations. He claims that *la langue* is essentially a social institution, organized by a set of logical conventions that are by nature interpersonal rather than subjective; therefore subjective, non-conceptional thought can *not* automatically be communicated by conventional associations of an arbitrary kind.[19] Instead, the subjective aspects of thought are communicated by means of associations that are essentially *non-arbitrary.*

> Since language is fundamentally intellectual it cannot communicate emotion except by means of an interplay of implicit associations. The signs of a language are arbitrary both in form (*signifiant*) and in content (*signifié*). So these associations stem either from the *signifiant*—so as to create a sensory impression—or from the *signifié* thereby transforming the concept into a mental image.[20]

These implicit associations, which give a sign its expressive potential, are based on relations which are exterior to the arbitrary and conventional relations of language. They arise *not* from the social contract of linguistic communication, but rather from relations that are assumed to be 'natural': i.e. relations between sounds or between thoughts that are perceived by the person independently of his knowledge of a language. Whereas the conceptual aspect of thought depends, as we have seen, on the structure of language, these implicit, affective relations are not established by linguistic fiat but according to similarities perceived in the

[19]Bally 1952, p. 92.
[20]Bally 1952, p. 83.

minds of the interactants. It is only here that Bally, otherwise a strict Saussurian, concedes any validity to the classical, anti-conventionalist theory of language advocated by Cratylus. It is important that the relation between *signifiant* and *signifié* remains arbitrary, according to Bally. The non-arbitrary, mimetic association characteristic of expressivity connects either the *signifiant* to a 'sound-impression' or the *signifié* to a 'mental-image'. The conventional, arbitrary relation between *signifiant* and *signifié* does not disappear. No matter how great the affective dominant, the conceptual aspect of the sign remains. Should it disappear, the expression would no longer be linguistic (as 'linguistic' implies 'conventional') but would become purely mimetic. Therefore, Bally is not claiming that expressivity abolishes or reduces the arbitrary nature of the sign. Instead, he seems to say that communication can be achieved, that is, the speaker's thought can be transmitted, *concurrently*, by more than one method. The greater the affective dominant of an expression, the less important the conventional relation between expression-form and concept and so the smaller the role of arbitrarity, but a role which is filled, all the same.

> I am claiming that linguistic expressivity...attaches either a sensory impression or a mental image to a concept, thereby veiling or concealing the concept while at the same time evoking it. Expressivity to this extent diminishes the role of arbitrary signs.[21]

It should be repeated that a 'diminished role' for arbitrarity is not the same thing as *reducing* the arbitrariness of the relation. In every linguistic sign a concept is evoked by the arbitrary relation between *significant* and *signifie*; but the more expressive a sign is the less important this particular process is to the communication achieved.

Thus along with their different conceptions of thought, Bally and the surrogationalist also disagree on how they think thought is communicated. Grafted on to the essential function of the communication of concepts by the relation of *signifiant* to *signifié*, argues Bally, is a quite different—but not independent—communicative process accounting for the communication of non-conceptual thought. The surrogationalist, Bally might insist, gives us no idea of how anything but pure logical concepts might be communicated. Asserting the importance of non-conceptual thought, Bally proposes to explain how it may be communicated with the same signs that are used to communicate conceptual thought: viz. the system of signs in *la langue*.

Expressivity and *la langue*

This raises an important question concerning Bally's notions of expressivity and communication: if the affective aspects of thought are communicated by an inter-

[21]Bally 1952, p. 89.

play of associations that are neither arbitrary nor conventional, then in what way is the study of expressivity in communication a study of *la langue*? As we shall see, this idea is relevant to all theories of structural stylistics. Either one explains stylistic effects by pointing to certain characteristics of *la langue* which exhibit a potential for the communication of expressivity, or one is forced to look elsewhere for the source of these effects. Bally's position on this question is most illuminating.

La langue was seen in Saussurian theory as constituting a set of social conventions, linking expression-forms with meanings in a purely arbitrary manner. But if stylistics is to be the study of the communication of the expressive aspects of thought by way of associations that are non-conventional and non-arbitrary, then it would seem that it is looking in the wrong domain for its 'object' of analysis. Surely the proper domain for the situation of such a process is in *parole* or in Saussure's notion of *langage*, rather than in *langue*. It is apparent that Bally's theory is highly structured by his notion of the dialectic of interaction. Language, communication, thought, and interaction are divided into pairs of contrastive characteristics. These oppose the personal to the inter-personal, the individual to the social, sentiment to concept, the non-arbitrary (or 'motivated') to the arbitrary, the non-conventional to the conventional, *parole* to *langue*. It would appear that the description and analysis that Bally gives of expressivity should unquestionably classify it in the former of each of the pairs of domains. Yet this was not Bally's opinion.

> Is a language therefore unable of its accord, to express emotions, desires, and the will ? We know quite well that it can.[22]

Bally did not ignore this important question; whether he answered it satisfactorily is another matter. Much of his paper 'Mecanisme de l'expressivité' deals with the question of whether expressivity has its source in the communication situation, or in *le langage*, or in *la langue*. His conclusion is that the expressivity of a speech act can arise from any one (or more than one) of these three, but that stylistics should properly be the study of expressivity in *la langue*.

> It is easily seen that the more conceptual signs of the language have associated to them expressive synonyms. If it is a question of vocabulary, compare: *He is going to die* with *He is lost; It is very pretty* with *It is stunning; My tooth hurts very much* with *My tooth is killing me* ... The emotion expressed by these forms actually belongs to them. It is part of the forms themselves. This is proof that there is no need to imagine a particular situation or to add supplementary context in order to discover their expressivity.[23]

Bally's case for claiming that expressive effects have their source in *la langue*

[22]Bally 1952, p. 82.
[23]Bally 1952, p. 82.

seems to rest on two crucial points. First, many expressive signs have become socialized. Their expressive effects are not due to an original, conscious use of them by an individual in a particular situation. Rather, these effects 'belong' to the signs by way of social convention. Their expressive content is invariant from situation to situation, use to use, speaker to speaker. In other words, the stylistic effect is associated to the sign which produces it in a conventional and invariant way just as is the sign's conceptual content.

Furthermore, according to the Saussurian conception of *la langue*, what is communicated by means that are available to all members of the linguistic community is, by definition, linguistic. That is, it is inherent to *la langue*. This principle does not have to conflict with the position that affective thought is communicated by means of an 'interplay of implicit associations'. Bally means to distinguish between expressivity in *parole*, when such an implicit association results from a ('one-off') creative use of language by the speaker, and expressivity in *la langue*. In the latter the 'interplay of associated ideas' is, so to speak, crystallized by use; that is, due to frequent use it has become conventionalized into *la langue*. For example, the expression *kick the bucket* has an expressive content that, due to its socialization, has become part of the language. When it is used for a particular expressive effect, no originality or creativity on the part of speaker or hearer is involved. The potential it has to evoke a mental image is independent of context and interlocutor. The expressive-content which it evokes comes automatically, in the same way as does a concept. The only difference is that the relation between the expressive-form and its affective content is motivated; while the relation between form and concept is arbitrary. Conventionalization is not seen to affect this distinction. The principle underlying this first point is as follows: something that is inter-subjectively available to all speakers at all times must belong to the means which they habitually employ to achieve communication. That is: language 'gives' us what we 'get' from communication. In the following chapters we will see that the interpretation of this principle is an important factor in the evolution of stylistic theory.

This brings us to the second point in Bally's justification for studying expressivity in *la langue*. That a particular sign provides an expressive effect is due to the fact that, in the minds of the speaker and hearer, that sign contrasts with another sign which is similar in intellectual content but has little or no expressive content.

> . . . a sign which becomes part of the language obeys the law which Saussure claims to be at the base of every system of signs: the law of opposition. The sign is understood and perceived not on its own but in relation to the other signs of the system. There is, in particular, a constant opposition, in the minds of speakers, between what is expressive and what is not.[24]

Hence, a sign with an 'affective dominant' is also part of the holistic system of *la langue*.

[24]Bally 1952, p. 96.

The Saussurian point of view sees the language user's knowledge of his language as consisting of an implicit ordering of linguistic features in relation to one another. Knowing how a particular sign is similar to and/or unlike the other signs of the language is, under this view, the possession of all the relevant *linguistic* knowledge about that sign. In this way, according to Bally, the free communication of the expressive effect of a sign depends upon the language-user's recognition of the opposition between that sign and other signs, one or more of which is not expressive. This contrast, sensed by the language-user, emphasizes the affective content of the sign. Equally, the similarity and dissimilarity between an expressive sign and certain other expressive signs indicates the characteristics of its expressive content. Accordingly, every sign of the language is said to have its content—both intellectual and expressive content—by opposition to the other signs of the language.

> Linguistic symbols only have signification and only evoke an effect by virtue of a general reaction of all the elements of the language.[25]

The reasoning underlying this second point incorporates a contradiction. If the value that an affective expression has is due to its opposition to the other expressions in the language, then what is the role of the 'interplay of associated ideas'? It appears that the Saussurian definition of a sign's value conflicts with Bally's account of the value of an expression with an affective dominant. That is, it cannot both be that (1) an expression has an affective value due to its conventionalized capacity to evoke a certain emotion, and that (2) it has that value due to its contrastive relations with the other expressions in the system. To make sense of this reasoning, Bally would have to admit that a sign does have a positive affective value, but that the extension of that value is determined by the contrast between it and the values of the other signs in the system. This concession, however, would amount to abandoning Saussure's dictum that in language there are only differences without positive terms.

Bally calls the system of relations between expressive signs the *systeme expressif*. It is apparent, however, that the expressive system of a language is to be distinguished from the system of relations between its conceptual signs because the former is neither arbitrary nor purely differential. Bally asserts that the ultimate goal for the stylistic study of a language should be to reveal its system of expressive relations.

The method of analysis

Bally's belief that a *système expressif* is an integral part of *la langue* greatly influences his proposed method for stylistic analysis. If linguistic expressivity is

[25]Bally 1909, p. 22.

the result of a system of oppositions, then a method is required which focuses on revealing such oppositions, that is, by contrasting signs with other signs. At the same time, because the object of investigation is a system of signs all similarly characterized by an 'affective dominant', these signs must therefore be contrasted with each other. Bally states that the *système expressif* reflects the 'natural categories of thought'.[26] To show how the system of expressive signs mirrors these categories of thought, stylistics must also focus on the similarities between signs with an 'affective dominant'. Although it is perhaps a platitude to say that the study of similarities and dissimilarities is a most fundamental methodological principle of linguistic analysis in general, this does not mean that all linguists respond to this principle with the same practices. All depends on the criteria chosen for the recognition of similarities and dissimilarities. In this and the following chapters, one of our primary considerations will be to investigate how this principle is applied over the course of the development of 20th century stylistics.

Synonymity plays a major role in Bally's investigative procedure. Attributing synonymy to two signs is seen as a way of isolating, within their general communicational relevance, their shared conceptual content. This casts a light on their non-conceptual differences. It must be made clear what Bally means by 'synonymy'. He does not, for instance, hold that two linguistic forms can ever be *completely* synonymous. Still, the study of synonymous relations is at the very heart of his stylistic method. Although ruling out the possibility of complete synonymy, he nonetheless argues that the term 'synonym' may be applied loosely, for all practical purposes, to refer to expressions that seem, to common-sense, very similar in content. The laxity of the use of this term also permits him to avoid defining any specific criteria for synonymy. He claims that there is never any real difficulty in telling intuitively if two terms are similar in meaning and that he who questions such a subjective evaluation is really concerned about the technical attribution of 'complete synonymy'. But this does not exist.

Instead, accepting that no two terms are perfect synonyms, Bally builds his investigative procedure on the analysis of those ways in which partial synonyms differ in communicational content. He contends that, very often, the difference would be due to the affective content of one or both of the expressions.

> The investigation of the intellectual and affective characteristics of particular expressions is nothing but a comprehensive study of synonymy, in the broadest sense of that term.[27]

Having contrasted an expression with its partial synonyms, the differences revealed should be categorized according to whether they are predominantly in-

[26]Bally 1909, p. 140.
[27]Bally 1909, p. 140.

tellectual or predominantly affective. Furthermore, in the latter category, the differences in affective content may be further classified into various sub-categories. Nevertheless, Bally points out,[28] of all the characteristics which distinguish an expression from its synonyms, there is always one which predominates. The dominant characteristics of expressions are said to be classifiable according to general categories of content, categories which themselves reflect 'the formal categories of thought'. From these general categories we may deduce the system of expressive values.

Significantly, Bally's criterion for calling two terms 'synonymous' is exclusively what he calls similarity of 'intellectual content'. There is no consideration of the possibility that the affective content of expressions might be relevant to the question of their synonymity. Instead, synonymy is a purely 'logical' equivalence.

The development of this point of view may be seen in Bally's proposed method for the isolation of the affective content of an expression. This step in the investigation, a stage which is supposed to be preparatory to that of stylistic analysis proper, involves what Bally calls 'identification'. The goal of identification is to find for the expression under analysis a partial synonym, i.e. another expression which has the same intellectual content as the original expression. This synonym is called the 'term of identification'.

> Identification is a logical linguistic operation. Its aim is to distinguish predominantly conceptual modes of expression. By contrast, these will serve to reveal the affective characteristics of other expressions.[29]

One might object that this is begging the question since the next step is to compare this term of identification with the original expression in order to determine the latter's expressive content. But how can we choose that logically equivalent 'term of identification' unless we already know of each expression's content what to count as intellectual and what as affective?

Bally's method attempts to safeguard against this problem. First, one establishes a group of expressions synonymous with that under analysis. Then these synonyms are ordered according to the logical relation of genus and species. The most general of the terms is that labelled 'term of identification'. Bally claims that, by ordering the synonyms of the analysed expression according to such a format, one can be sure of choosing a term of identification whose content contains the essential conceptual (or intellectual) core of the other synonyms.

> The goal of detailed analysis will be unattainable unless particular expressions are first grouped around one expression possessing the fundamental

[28]Bally 1909, p. 140.
[29]Bally 1909, p. 105.

meaning which is common to all the other synonyms. In addition, this expression must present the core meaning with a maximum of conceptual objectivity and a minimum of affect.[30]

In other words, it is claimed that the general term of identification may differ in meaning from the other synonyms in the group but that this difference should not be 'fundamental'. Here again, the question, before put off, is begged. How do we determine which are the 'fundamental' characteristics of an expression's content? Bally seems to be caught straddling the fence between logic and subjective evaluation. Do we know what the fundamental characteristics are because of intuition, or because ordering the terms according to relations of genus and species guarantees that the superordinate term will always contain all the fundamental characteristics of the subordinate? Or, indeed, is the expression 'fundamental characteristics' simply defined in terms of the genus-species relation such that, by definition, the fundamental characteristics of a subordinate term are all those included in the superordinate term? But then, how do we distinguish genus from species?

Bally himself does not raise any of these questions. One might assume that he found his method sufficiently straightforward, so that answers to such questions, as regards the analysis of any particular expression, could always be found through introspection. Furthermore, he did propose a second method for checking on the logical character of the term of identification.

> To say that one has succeeded in identifying a particular expression, it is necessary that...for all practical purposes, the two expressions be substitutable for each other without affecting logical content.[31]

Here then arises another criterion that the term of identification must satisfy: it must be substitutable for the expression under analysis without affecting logical content. 'But', the critic will ask, 'how can we tell if the logical content is or is not changed in substitution without first being able to determine what is and what is not the logical content?' In a sense, in order to be able to carry out such an operation we would have to already have the information that we are seeking to establish: viz. what part of the meaning of the expression is affective and what part conceptual. The justification that Bally seems to offer is that we can already be sure of a purely intellectual relation between the term of identification and the expression under analysis since it was established by the logical operation of genus and species. But this, as we have seen, is a circular argument.

The problem regarding the particular process of 'identification' seems to be the following: in order to isolate the affective content of an expression, the exact

[30]Bally 1909, p. 107.
[31]Bally 1909, p. 109.

intellectual content must first be determined. To do this, however, one will need a criterion to distinguish the affective aspects of the content from the intellectual content. But if this criterion is already available then there is no need of the process of 'identification' since the criterion can already distinguish affective from intellectual content. If this criterion is not available, then the process of identification cannot proceed unless the question it is supposed to answer—regarding the separation of affective from intellectual content—is begged from the very start.

A more general problem arises from seeing communicational content as consisting of 'parts', or of different types of characteristics inherent to the 'thing' that is the content. This notion, as we have seen, arises in turn from Bally's and Saussure's concept of *la langue* as a system of relations. These must be relations between 'things', if perhaps abstract, ephemeral things. Bally stretches to the breaking point this notion of a holistic system of language. By recognizing the many functions that language serves in communication, he has uncovered the heterogeneity of communication. But, a convinced Saussurian, he argues that nothing can be communicated that does not have the teleological source of its communication in the structure of a language. Hence, in the language itself must lie the explanation of its variety of functions. The structure of a language must reflect the heterogeneity of communication. In order to account for its functions in interaction, the system of *la langue* is augmented with structures and types of content. Each aspect of content represents a contribution, by the language, to one of its communicational functions. It is revealing that in order to account for this heterogeneity, Bally must speak of more than one system of content, and within them, sub-systems.

But such a reductionist view of communicational function (i.e. assuming that the source of what we 'get' in communication must lie in the structure of the language) creates a difficult problem for the linguist or stylistician intent on identifying the different functional 'parts' or aspects of content. He will always require a criterion for establishing what counts as one aspect and what does not. This is an especially worrying dilemma for the Saussurian structuralist because it forces him to treat content as a positive entity. If content is treated as a question only of differences, with no positive terms, then there can be no question of talking about 'parts' or aspects of differences. Pure negativity is not divisible.

As regards affective content, however, Bally has been shown not to adopt the differential principle. Affective content is positivized by the conventional interplay of associated ideas. That is, the affective content of an expression does not just consist in the manifold contrasts between that expression and other expressions in the system. Contrast may regulate its form or extension, but affective content still has a positive substance: viz. a mental image or a sensory-impression.

But the problem of criteria still arises. There is no criterion by which the sameness or difference of two aspects of communicational content may be determined. How can we tell if two expressions, e.g. *chick* and *broad,* are equally derogatory? Is one more informal or less vulgar than the other? On what criteria could we base such decisions? The classification that is required to reveal the expressive system of a language relies on the ability of the stylistician to provide an answer to just this type of question. But, on the assumption that affective content belongs to particular expressions, the criterion-less investigator has no way of determining either (a) what that content is, or (b) whether the content of one expression is the same as or different than the content of another expression. The goal of revealing the expressive system of a language would appear to be unattainable.

Bally provides no door by which the stylistician may exit from this dilemma. But this does not mean that he abandons the project. Instead, he appears to rely on his own intuition as the relevant criterion with which to differentiate and categorize the affective contents of expressions. This is no help to the stylistician who wants to continue Bally's investigations. There is no guarantee that what one investigator senses to be an intuitive difference in affective content will strike another investigator in just the same way. A feminist, for instance, might find *broad* to be insulting in a way that *chick* is not. There is no assurance that the chauvinist will agree. Everyone could construct his own expressive system.

Evidently, this dilemma stems from the impossibility of observing the stylistic contents on which the crucial analysis of the expression-plane depends. It might be possible to observe privately the experience of this content, but each person could never tell if what he privately observes is the same as what someone else privately observes, or even (as Wittgenstein remarks) whether what they privately observe now is the same as what they privately observed two days ago. Bally seems to assume that we all do experience the same pattern of samenesses and differences of communicational content, but he does not say how to determine what that pattern is. It may be claimed, as deductive premisses, (a) that affective contents are inter-subjective, (b) that they 'belong' to particular expressions, (c) that native language-users all (at least implicitly) recognize this, and (d) that this is why the communication of the affective aspects of thought works. But when it comes down to applying these claims to the investigation of the empirical details of particular expressions, the crucial inter-subjectivity of the contents seems to dissolve in unsupportable, multi-subjective intuitions.

The system of expressivity

Having 'isolated' the affective content of an expression by the method outlined above, Bally then classifies this content under one of a set of categories of expressive functions. These categories are drawn from Bally's notion of communicational interaction. Still, due to the teleological relation between communication and language, these categories are supposed to be inherent to the object described, i.e. to the system of oppositions that is *la langue*.

A general division is drawn between 'natural effects' and 'evocative effects'. The latter refer to the socially categorizing effects of language; that is, to as effects of 'register' or of regional or occupational 'dialect'. These effects are concerned with the fact that certain expressions, intonations, accents, syntagmatic patterns, etc., 'evoke' their typical situation of occurrence. By virtue of this, the language a speaker uses is said to be socially classified as that of a factory-worker, a middle-class Parisian, a journalist, and so on. The expressive difference intuitively sensed between these aspects of language would be said to reflect their different evocative effects. Bally proposes that the way to identify particular effects of this kind is to compare the register-particular expression with a synonymous expression of *la langue commune*. This, of course, presupposes that it is possible to identify some such thing as the *la langue commune* of a particular linguistic community, in contrast to all other forms of *la langue*. Here again, one is in need of specific criteria.

If, at this general categorical level of expressivity, evocative effects may be seen to reflect the influence of social forces on language, the other general category, natural effects, concerns those effects resulting from the influence of the other interactional pole: personal expression.

> Natural effects have to do with the agreable or disagreable impression we sense upon hearing a certain word. . . . Also, when an expression causes us to perceive a concept with particular vividness, this is a natural effect. The same goes for when an expression awakens in us an impression of beauty, of delicateness, of grace....[32]

Within the category of natural effects two further subclasses are drawn which also reflect Bally's notion of the dialectic of interaction. First the subjective aspect of thought, which is communicated by natural effects, may be concerned with the speaker's orientation to his addressee(s). In modern terminology this would be called 'recipient-design'. Bally claims that a language provides ways for the speaker to communicate his subjective evaluation of those with whom he is speaking. For example, this potential is reflected in the different variety of language one uses in speaking to a child as compared to when one's addressee is a social superior.

> In this case, we represent the social condition of the person as lower or higher than ourselves and especially the relations which exist between that person and us and which may or may not distance us from them.[33]

[32]Bally 1909, p. 167.
[33]Bally 1909, p. 9.

It should be noted here that 'recipient-design' is an indirect social effect on language; 'indirect' because it is modulated by the speaker's recognition of social relations. On the other hand, evocative effects do not presuppose the speaker's recognition of the content communicated. The latter are, in this sense, less subjective and more directly social.

The orientation to social relations as perceived by the speaker is to be contrasted with those expressive effects representing sentiments of a non-social nature: i.e. desire, anger, disgust, etc. These more purely subjective natural effects are concerned with the speaker's evaluation of the topic of his utterance.

> ...here the effect has its source in the way in which the thought is presented, in the perspective from which the expression makes us see the thought.[34]

So, while the 'recipient-design' effects reflect the speaker's subjective impression of the social nature of the speech situation, the 'topic-evaluative' effects reflect his impression of the subject of his discourse. Furthermore, the 'topic' or 'subject' of the speaker's talk is, for Bally, that which is expressed directly by the intellectual content of the words used.

It follows then that the 'topic-evaluative' effect of an expression comments on the intellectual content of that expression, reflecting the speaker's feelings toward the 'true' or 'linguistic' meaning of his utterance. Here we see the theoretical motif, frequently adopted by modern stylisticians and literary critics, of the self-referring sign. In this way, both types of Bally's natural effects may be seen to concern an implicit reference to the speech act: either to the intellectual content ('linguistic meaning', 'logical content', 'cognitive meaning', etc.) of the utterance or to the utterance's social context.

Finally, Bally argues that the comment made on either situation or topic by the natural effect may be seen as tending towards one of two contrastive poles. Natural effects are either favourable or unfavourable.

Although Bally does indeed speak of other categories of expressivity and qualifies the application of some of those already outlined, the following model will suffice for our present expository purposes.

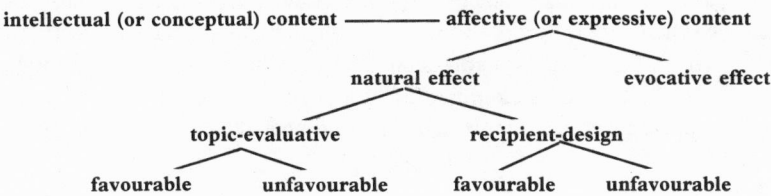

---

[34]Bally 1909, p. 167.

It must not be forgotten that Bally does not claim that a sign has only one type of effect. On the contrary, one and the same sign can produce a variety of effects, but the object of stylistics, according to Bally, is the study of the dominant effect of any particular sign or group of signs.

In parenthesis, it should be remarked that, within the categories of expressivity, Bally does not include literary or poetic effects. This is an important distinction because Bally's followers came to regard these effects as central to the explanatory task of stylistics. But Bally excludes the study of literary effects from the domain of stylistics because those effects are supposedly the result of the conscious and voluntary manipulation of language by the author. Stylistics, on the other hand, should be the study of the ordinary, spontaneous use of language.[35] What appears to be so blatantly abnormal in the literary use of language is the concentration on the means rather than on the ends of expression.

> The difference lies in the motive and in the intention. The result is different because the intended effect is not the same. That which is an end for the poet is, for the ordinary man, only a means. For the ordinary man, linguistic processes only serve to exteriorize his impressions, his desires, his impulses. Once this is accomplished, he has achieved his goal. But the poet aspires to transform the ordinary into the beautiful.[36]

Bally claims that the poet's intention is contrary to the natural social function of language. For the ordinary language-user the intention to produce beauty

> is given little priority in relation to the exacting demands put upon language in its natural, social function.[37]

Bally illustrates this distinction with an analogy. In war-games armies act as if they were fighting a war but do not attempt to accomplish the same ends. That is, what are generally the means of the action become its ends.

> ...while the act retains its emotive force, without which its purpose could not be achieved, it detaches itself from the person who performs it. The soldier becomes an actor in a role.[38]

While the above outlined categories of expressivity are admirably clear and simple, nevertheless Bally proposes no method by which one may categorize the effect or effects of a particular expression. Nor does he explain how one might tell which of a sign's effects is dominant. The stylistician who is interested in this taxonomic approach is left disturbingly ill-equipped to attain the prize which awaits him.

[35]Bally 1952, p. 28ff.
[36]Bally 1952, p. 29.
[37]Bally 1909, pp. 179-80
[38]Bally 1952, p. 29.

Evidently what is needed is a publicly observable criterion with which to judge the relations between different effects. Linguistics proper is fortunate to have such a practical criterion. The conceptual sameness of two expressions can usually be determined, for all practical purposes, by seeing if they may be substituted in the same contexts without affecting truth-conditions. More practical still is the criterion of the dictionary. Stylistics, however, does not have the benefit of such criteria. So, while linguistics is able to analyse the substantive differences in the expression-plane from the perspective of sameness and difference of meaning, stylistics, on the other hand, is crippled by the lack of such a criterion.

At least, Bally's Saussurian analysis of style would lead one to this conclusion. His taxonomic proposals appear quite speculative due to the absence of a firm criterial perspective. They are as firmly grounded in his own intuition as alternative proposals would be grounded in the intuition of another, rival investigator. Stylistics will not achieve scientific respectability on the basis of such unverifiable speculations.

But the taxonomic description of style is not the only possible approach. Successors to Bally soon came to the conclusion that it might be possible to preserve Bally's original ambition—i.e. to found a structural analysis of style—without necessarily being caught in the same dilemma.

3

Jakobson and the Poetic Function of Language

It is perhaps unwise, if not uncommon, to speak of 'schools' of stylistics. Few stylisticians agree on a theoretical definition of the term 'style' and fewer still on the correct methods of stylistic analysis. This is probably due—as was remarked in the first chapter—to the composite nature of the concept of style: an amalgam of psychological, sociological, literary, and linguistic notions which are both common-sensical and 'theoretical' in their origins and uses. It should therefore be no surprise that there are few 'schools' of stylistics in the sense of groups of researchers who all investigate the same phenomena using the same methods. And this is true in spite of the fact that the name given to the 'object' of the stylistician's investigations—'style'—and to the investigations themselves—'stylistics'—often remain invariant. Consequently, even though two stylisticians might find themselves using the same terms, what one calls 'style' the other may say is not an objectively identifiable linguistic phenomenon at all, but merely a figment created by the first stylistician's use of the term 'style'. As a result of this perhaps unavoidable epistemological dialectic between realism and nominalism, so common to the characteristic language-games of the social sciences, stylistic theories are often couched in idiosyncratic definitions and terminology which make comparison difficult. Thus the historian or critic of stylistic theory, looking for an underlying constancy of theoretical development, has set himself a difficult task.

In spite of this general situation, it will nonetheless be maintained that certain equivalences between theories may be established. Such equivalences are often due to the work of one man. In linguistics such a man would be Saussure, and the work, his *Cours de linguistique generale*. Few linguists agree with the totality of his theory; indeed, few linguists today would claim that Saussure's theory forms a coherent whole; but fewer still would disagree that his influence was and still is immeasurably great. His theory has become a point of reference, a context against which another linguist's theory is contrasted. Individually, his thoughts on language reappear in countless linguistic theories. That these thoughts are often found to be unsatisfactory is of no great importance. The point is that linguists seem to feel obliged to deal with them.

In stylistic theory, a similar degree of influence has been attained by the work of Roman Jakobson. It may be true that there are far fewer works on style, but even in this smaller field the footnotes and bibliographical references to Jakobson

appear as frequently as do those to Saussure in linguistics. But this is a more surprising fact than it otherwise might be because Jakobson has never written of
himself as a stylistician. In his works which have had such a great impact on contemporary stylistic theory, he does not even mention the word 'style'. Instead
Jakobson's influence stems from his writings related to poetics,¹ or, the study of
literarity in poetic language.

Bally and Jakobson

That this theory has become the touchstone of structural stylistics would not
give the founder of modern stylistics, Charles Bally, great satisfaction. Bally explicitly excluded the study of literary language from the domain of stylistics. But
stylistics has greatly changed since the appearance in 1909 of the *Traité de
stylistique française*. Bally's own influence in the field seems to have greatly
diminished if, superficially, one only takes into account citations and footnotes.
But, as we shall see, much of his thought on the role of style in communication
has had a profound, if rarely acknowledged, effect on modern stylistic theory. It
would not be difficult to argue that stylistics today, if not entirely the discipline
that Bally had envisaged, is the direct descendent of the theory originally
presented in the *Traité*.

To understand Jakobson's influence on the course of stylistics, one must
understand what he felt to be the object of his own investigations. In his most influential paper, 'Linguistics and Poetics', which was presented as a 'concluding
statement: from the viewpoint of linguistics' at the *Conference on Style* held at In-
diana University in 1958, he argued as follows:

> Poetics deals primarily with the question, 'What makes a verbal message a
> work of art?'...the main subject of poetics is the *differentia specifica* of verbal
> art in relation to other arts and in relation to other kinds of verbal behavior.¹

For the stylisticians of the Jakobsonian school, the study of the verbal message as
a work of art *is* the study of style. In this way the object of stylistic investigation
has been altered since Bally's day. But this is not entirely due to Roman Jakobson.

In fact the field of stylistics, such as Bally envisaged it, did not remain
unaltered for very long. The first change consisted in the restriction of the domain of investigation to that of literary style. This was accomplished, against
Bally's own wishes, by his followers and students in France: e.g. Marouzeau,
Cressot, Guiraud. For these men, literary language not only exploited the
potential for expressivity inherent—as Bally pointed out—in any language, but
represented the epitome of the expressive use of language. Paradoxically,

<hr/>

¹Jakobson 1960, p. 350.

literature, for the disciples of Bally, became the focal point of stylistic analysis for precisely the same reasons that had prompted Bally to exclude it from stylistics. That is, in literature, the use of the stylistic function of language is both conscious and voluntary.[2] In this respect, Roman Jakobson's theory of poetics constituted a logical development from the stylistic theories of Bally's followers.

The second major development in stylistic theory since Bally concerned the expansion and schematization of his notion of the functions of language. This provided for the accommodation of the specific characteristics of literary style within a functional perspective on language. The resultant theory of the functions of language in communication, developed by Roman Jakobson, will be of primary interest to us in the present chapter. It will be seen that one of Jakobson's major contributions to modern stylistics lies in his efforts to determine the linguistic criteria which indicate the function that an utterance has in communication. This is essentially where Bally left off; after providing an interesting account of the function of language in communication he provided no method of analysis by which one could identify the function(s) of any particular expression. It is possible that this important break from the impressionism of Bally, pushing the linguistic method of analysis further into stylistics, constitutes the reason why Jakobson has acquired such an influence in the field.

Perhaps the most significant similarity between the theories of Bally and Jakobson—and this also accounts for Jakobson's revitalization of interest in linguistic stylistics—is that both can be seen to adhere to a general view which might be called 'linguistic reductionism'. Both theories carry the presupposition that a variety of aspects of communication, e.g. poeticity, expressivity, register, etc., may be explained in terms of an analysis of particular aspects of the language 'code'. (This expression is Jakobson's term for what Bally called *la langue.*) Jakobson and Bally believed (a) that the communicational relevance of speech, or of writing, could not be created *ex nihilo*; (b) that this relevance must have its source in some particular system of organized phenomena; and (c) that such a system could only be the language that is used for communication. According to this view the communicational relevance of an utterance must be due to the particular nature and organization of that utterance. In this way, Bally could approach the study of expressivity in communication purely by an analysis of similarities and contrasts between linguistic forms. Equally, Jakobson's study of the poetic function of a message focuses its analysis on the linguistic organization of that message. Neither of these views, however, should be seen as denying the role of situational factors in communication. On the contrary, their analysis of language is based upon a prior analysis of these factors. But what they do advocate is that a particular factor of the communication situation is only relevant

[2]cf. Cressot 1947, p. 3.

to the interpretation of an utterance if some particular *linguistic* feature of that utterance signals its relevance.

A related parallel may be drawn between the views held by Bally and Jakobson on the distinctiveness of verbal art. Bally claims that the stylistic effects of literary language are not due to the spontaneous use of language but result, instead, from the author's conscious and voluntary concentration on the means rather than on the ends of his expression. Jakobson, a student of the revolutionary Russian Formalist school of literary criticism, also argues that what is 'poetic' about poetic language is itself non-pragmatic. It has neither the expressive nor the referential function to communicate thoughts. Instead, it promotes a focus on the poetic utterance itself and on its lingustic properties. This also implies a concentration on the means rather than on the ends of language use.

> How does poeticity manifest itself? In the fact that the word is perceived as a word, not as a simple substitute for the object named, nor as an explosion of emotion.[3]

Furthermore, the theories of literary language which were formulated by Bally and Jakobson seem similar in that both related this part of their theories to a more general analysis of the functions of language in communication. A fundamental difference between these two theories is that Jakobson, with his highly schematized account of communication, is able to account for literary or poetic factors without exiling them, like Bally, beyond the descriptive reaches of the theory. For this reason, Jakobson's theory was able to revitalize the field of stylistics.

A structure superimposed on the message

A structuralist stylistic theory based on Jakobson's theory of poetics conceives of style, in the first instance, as a structure superimposed on a linguistic message. A (simplified) explanation of this point of view might say that a message with literary style is organized not only by its 'ordinary' linguistic structure—i.e. by what some linguists would call its grammar—but also by an arbitrary arrangement of some of the linguistic features into patterns and repetitions. The first, *a priori* structure—the grammar—is obligatory for any message. It is the grammar which gives a string of sounds a structure without which communication would be impossible. The second—superimposed—structure is the *a posteriori* stylistic structure. This is neither obligatory for any or every utterance nor vital to the referential function of the utterance. However, this does not preclude a possible contribution made by the superimposed structure to the communication of the utterance. The important point here is that this superimposed structure is, in a

[3]Jakobson 1973, p. 124.

sense, supplementary. An adherent to Jakobsonian stylistics, G-G. Granger, calls this process *surcodage* and identifies the distinction between the two organizing structures as relating to two types of codes relevant to the interpretation of the message: *a priori* for grammar, *a posteriori* for style.[4] Furthermore, Granger claims that the stylistic structure is imposed on the 'variable features of the code' (cf. the use of this expression in C.E. Osgood's article in the *Style in Language* collection)[5] rather than on the obligatory features. The variable features are those which are redundant, residual, or inessential as far as the communication of meaning by the message is concerned. In this sense the stylistic structure does not disrupt the essential meaning-producing function of the message.

> The enhancement of expression evidently consists, if not in reducing this residue to a minimum, then in treating it with a particular intention which constitutes its style.[6]

In other words, a message may acquire a second communicational function, besides that of transmitting meaning, as a result of a specific type of structure being superimposed on the variable features in its expression-plane. Its conceptual meaning is communicated due to the relation it bears to the rules of the language. Many of the expression-features, however, remain variable. If I utter a sentence with a high frequency of sibilants, this high frequency will not affect the meaning of the sentence because there is no rule of English which invariantly attaches a specific meaning to all sentences with a high frequency of sibilants. But this pattern of sibilants might give the sentence a secondary function, other than that of communicating meaning. It might, for instance, give it an expressive function. If these sibilants were combined with other suitable features, like raised voice and clipped terminal consonants, they might together help communicate the knowledge that I was angry. This would be in spite of the fact that the meaning of the sentence I uttered—determined by its relation to the rules of the language—gives no hint of that anger. The expressive function of that sentence—communicating the speaker's emotion—lies in a conceptually irrelevant, superimposed structure which patterns the variable features of the message. The reasoning from the principles of the bi-planar model should be clear: since the bi-planar model gives us linguistic structure by viewing language from the perspective of meaning, the view from the perspective of other communicational functions will have to reveal other structures as their causes.

The reader will here be reminded of Bally's distinction between the arbitrary relation linking *signifiant* to *signifie*, a relation determined by convention and essential to the communication of the sign, and the 'interplay of associated ideas'

---

[4]Granger 1968, p. 191.
[5]Osgood 1960, p. 293ff.
[6]Granger 1968, p. 122.

which characterises the communication of expressivity. These associations are based, according to Bally, not on the conventions of the language, but on extra-linguistic relations, and they do not alter, although they may diminish, the role of the primary, linguistic relation between *signifiant* and *signifie*. This parallel is of interest because it highlights the equal degree of respect held by the Jakobso-nians and Bally for the primacy of the linguistic sign. Style for the Jakobsonian structuralist, like style for Bally, (although the phenomena referred to by the common term may not be the same) does not disrupt the process of ordinary linguistic communication. It is for one a pattern superimposed upon the variable features of the message, which is itself already patterned according to the conven-tions of the language. For the other, it is a network of associated ideas that are related to, but specifically distinct from, the conventions of the language. Jakob-son aptly summarizes this shared perspective:

> Obviously we must agree with Sapir that, on the whole, 'ideation reigns supreme in language'. . . , but this supremacy does not authorize linguistics to disregard the 'secondary factors'.[7]

A further parallel may be drawn here to the distinction made in J.L. Austin's theory of language between the proposition expressed by an utterance and its il-locutionary force.[8] The proposition that is expressed by an utterance—like Bally's conventional relation between *signifiant* and *signifie*—is said to depend on the rules or conventions of the language. On the other hand, the illocutionary force that an utterance has depends upon a variety of extra-linguistic criteria relating to the context of the communication situation. These also may be con-ventional, as Strawson points out,[9] but the conventions in question would then be considered to be distinct from the conventions of the language. In each of these three theories (Jakobson's, Bally's, Austin's) the 'linguistic' function of a message is seen to be the communication of a meaning, but the message may have other functions too. The linguistic meaning is determined solely by virtue of the conventions of the language, independent of the context of utterance or of whatever communicative functions the utterance may serve. The style, literarity, or illocutionary force, although communicated by the very same message, is seen as supplementary to the invariant, conventional meaning. In the theories of Bally and Austin, this secondary effect supposedly springs from an extra-linguistic source, the communication situation. However, Bally, unlike Austin, felt that the language itself is permanently adapted to this constant pressure of situational requirements.

Jakobson is not forced to turn to extra-linguistic sources to explain the

[7]Jakobson 1960, p. 353.
[8]Austin 1962.
[9]Strawson 1971, p. 149ff.

phenomena of style. Instead, he attributes the source of the phenomena to a second, supplementary application to the utterance of the same conventions of language which give the utterance its primary structure. This re-application of linguistic conventions, by which the literary message acquires its superimposed structure or style, is not an easy notion to grasp. It can hardly be understood without a detailed analysis of Jakobson's notions of the functions of language, and specifically of that function which is said to characterize literary style: the poetic function.

The poetic function

Jakobson bases his account of the functions of language on what he considers to be 'the six constitutive factors of any speech event'.

> The ADDRESSER sends a MESSAGE to the ADDRESSEE. To be operative the message requires a CONTEXT referred to ('referent' in another somewhat ambiguous nomenclature), seizable by the addressee, and either verbal or capable of being verbalized; a CODE fully, or at least partially, common to the addresser and addressee (or in other words, to the encoder and decoder of the message); and finally, a CONTACT, a physical channel and psychological connection between the addresser and the addressee, enabling both of them to enter and stay in communication. All these factors inalienably involved in verbal communication may be schematized as follows:

$$\begin{array}{c} \text{CONTEXT} \\ \text{ADDRESSER} \text{---------------------------} \text{MESSAGE} \text{---------------------------} \text{ADDRESSEE} \\ \text{CONTACT} \\ \text{CODE} \end{array}$$

> Each of these six factors determines a different function of language.[10]

Jakobson claims that the function of an utterance depends on its 'orientation to' one or more of these six constitutive factors of the speech event. For instance, an utterance's orientation toward the context would mean that it has a referential function. Similarly, an orientation towards the code of the utterance constitutes the metalinguistic function of that utterance. As a result, a parallel schema may be established of the six functions of language, each one denoting an orientation towards a particular factor of the speech event. Jakobson's schema of these functions is as follows:

$$\begin{array}{lll} & \text{REFERENTIAL} & \\ \text{EMOTIVE} & \text{POETIC} & \text{CONATIVE[11]} \\ & \text{PHATIC} & \\ & \text{METALINGUAL} & \end{array}$$

[10]Jakobson 1960, p. 353.
[11]Jakobson 1960, p. 357.

One is reminded here of Bally's notion of the various functions of language. His recipient-design features would surely count as an example of an orientation to the addressee of the speech event, in other words, of the conative function. Similarly, what he refers to as the intellectual content of an expression, as compared to its expressive content, would in Jakobson's terms be characterized by the distinction between the referential and emotive functions of a language. But the other functions identified by Jakobson do not have parallels in Bally's work.

Despite Bally's insights into the psychological and sociological aspects of communicative interaction, the distinctions he draws between different *types* of these aspects do not seem based on any identifiable criteria. This in turn leads to the difficulty the analyst faces in trying to determine whether an expression's affective content is best characterized as e.g. an evocative effect, or recipient-design, or a natural effect, etc. In this respect Jakobson's theory of the functions of language seems to be more soundly based since each identified function of language is determined by its orientation to a specific factor of the speech event. Consequently, the study of the functions of language at least comes closer to having some distinguishing criteria of identification. Furthermore, Jakobson proposes, at least for some of the functions, a method of determining, from the linguistic evidence of an utterance, which is its major function. This results in a method for the analysis of non-cognitive aspects of language-use that is on a more empirical footing than that proposed by Bally.

The poetic function, of interest to us here because it is said to account for the literarity, or style, of an utterance, is 'the set (*Einstellung*) toward the MESSAGE as such, focus on the message for its own sake'.[12] This is perhaps one of the most frequently quoted phrases in modern stylistic theory, and yet its meaning is not easily grasped. Do we not always focus on the message in communication? In what way is this 'focus' different? And what does 'for its own sake' mean? Perhaps these puzzling questions may be clarified by situating this description of the poetic function within Jakobson's descriptions of the other functions.

Jakobson uses a number of terms interchangeably with 'focus on' when speaking of the relation between message and speech situation. These terms include: 'orientation toward', 'set toward', 'accent on', and the German *Einstellung*. In the French edition of the article, translated from the original English by N. Ruwet, the terms employed are *orientation vers, visee de, l'accent mis sur,* and *centré sur*. Nowhere, however, is this crucial concept—referring to the relation between message and situation—ever explicitly defined.

E. Holenstein, in his book *Roman Jakobson's Approach to Language: Phenomenological Structuralism,* argues that the relation between message and situational factor—expressed by the terms 'focus on', 'set towards', and so on—should be interpreted within the context of phenomenological theory. According to this explanation each of the six factors may be seen as relevant in a

[12]Jakobson 1960, p. 356.

particular way to the in-context interpretation of the message. For example, *What a rotten day* might be seen in relation to the speaker's (or 'addresser's') role in the speech event, e.g. as an expression of his disappointment with the weather, or of his anger, etc. This constitutes a possible emotive function for the message and, as such, is reminiscent of Bally's notion of expressivity. The message could also be interpreted specifically in its relation to the hearer, e.g. as a suggestion that the plans he had made have to be abandoned because of the weather. Relating to what Jakobson calls the context or referent, this message may simply be seen as fulfilling the role of a description of the weather, apart from any considerations of the addresser or addressee's personal commitment to the utterance. Or it might be seen as a platitude uttered between neighbours meeting on the street, having no real descriptive, conative, or emotive function, but simply that of establishing verbal contact between speaker and hearer. (Jakobson gives as an example of a message with a phatic function or orientation to the contact: *Hello, do you hear me?* and the reply, *um-hum!*[13]) With a metalinguistic function, this message could be used, for instance, to explain by example the use of the word *rotten* to a foreigner or child. In this way the focus of the message would be on the code of the language; i.e. the interpretation of the message is seen as relating to that particular factor of the speech event. Finally a message with a poetic function is said to focus on itself in its role as a message. This superficially confusing notion is, in fact, not very different from Bally's notion of the aesthetic concentration on the means of expression rather than on its ends. But before we turn to what constitutes the focus of a message on itself, we should first investigate further this notion of 'focus'.

We have seen that the 'focus' or 'set' of a message determines which factor of the speech event is the most relevant to the interpretation of the message, i.e. which of the possible interpretations outlined above is to be taken as the most relevant one (although not necessarily the only relevant one) for a particular occasion of its use. According to Holenstein, this is related to the phenomenological notion of *apperception*, that is, to the notion of the interpretive role of the subject in perception. To the phenomenologist, perception is not a passive but an active event to which the perceiver contributes as much as does the object perceived. As an example of this, Holenstein refers to Husserl's writings with which, indeed, Jakobson was quite familiar.[14]

> The starting point of the theory of apperception is the observation that the same objects can apparently be differently apprehended. To use Husserl's favorite illustration, we suddenly grasp as letters the same figures that we first held to be arabesques. The doctrine of apperception concludes that a purely objective investigation is an illusion. The study of an object should be linked with methodological reflection on the orientation, point of view, or mode of apprehension of the subject.[15]

[13]Jakobson 1960, p. 355.
[14]cf. Holenstein 1976, p. 50ff and interview with Jakobson in *Cahiers Cistre*, 5.
[15]Holenstein 1976, p. 51.

For the phenomenologist the notion of apperception is especially relevant to an understanding of the constitution of the linguistic message *as* an object of perception. Without the interpretive contribution by the subject (the language-user) to the act of perceiving the utterance, the latter would be no more than a string of sounds. There is a great distance between our perception of a sentence of our own language and our perception of an utterance of a language we have never heard before. Language-users are not like human spectrographs. Their perception of an utterance of their own language is determined by more than purely acoustic characteristics, and so can never be wholly objective. If the contributory role of the language-user is taken into account, the utterance may be seen as more than a string of sounds. Instead, it will be perceived as a configuration of phonemes, morphemes, words, phrases, etc. The language-user's perception of a verbal string is heavily influenced by this possibility of his implicit recognition of it *as an utterance of his language*. According to this theory, then, the categories of grammar are seen as reflecting the criteria which govern this interpretive structuring of the apperceptual transformation of a sound-string into an utterance of a language. This discussion—already suggested in our introductory examination of the criteria for the attribution of 'sameness' of form and meaning—is central to the longstanding argument between 'etic' and 'emic' approaches to linguistics, an argument in which Jakobson has played a conspicuous role in supporting the 'emic' or criterial point of view.

Of specific relevance to the theory of the functions of the linguistic message is the following: In its constitution as a social object, the string of sounds—which, due to the phenomenon of apperception, is seen as having a grammatical structure—concurrently undergoes a second, 'emic' analysis by the language-user. This second analysis results in the attribution of what could be called a 'situational function' to the utterance. Jakobson's theory of the functions of language may be seen as attempting to account for the nature of this second level of analysis. In this way, the language-user perceives a string of sounds not only as an utterance of his language, but also as a functional part of the communication situation. Similar to Husserl's figures which we suddenly grasp as letters, the verbal string is grasped as two different types of things: as an utterance of the language and as a particular type of communicational event. It is important to recognize that the role of apperception is here double. Two influences organize the perceptual activity of the language-user in such a way that the speech-string is not just perceived *tout court*, but is twice 'seen as': i.e. it is perceived in relation to two separate points of view: grammar and situational function.

As we have seen in the case of *What a rotten day*, the perceptual object in question—a linguistic message—may be interpreted in a variety of different ways. But, according to this theory, it does not alter its status as an utterance of the language (English, in this case) whether it is seen as a description of the weather or as an expression of the speaker's discontent or as a hint to the hearer, etc.

Secondly, and this is an essential principle of the theory, the focus of the message determines *inter-subjectively*—i.e. for all interlocutors—which of these roles in the communication situation the message should be seen in fulfilling. In the same way that the first 'set' towards the grammar relates the message to an interpretive structure that is inter-subjective—in the sense of activating, to all intents and purposes, the same set of criteria for speaker and hearer(s)—the second 'set' toward the situation acquires this inter-subjectivity by means of the orienting focus of the message. The focus determines what factor in the speech event is most relevant to the interpretation of the message. It assures, to a degree sufficient for the purposes of the communication, that speaker and hearer(s) take the same perspective on the speech event and on the message's role in it. Thus, in the speech event, as it is pictured in this phenomenologico-structural account, the fundamentally subjective phenomenon of apperception acquires a sufficient degree of inter-subjectivity to enable communication between addresser and addressee(s).

Jakobson, as both Holenstein and Granger point out, acknowledges the affinities between this account of the process of linguistic communication and the theory of 'semiotic' developed by the Harvard philosopher C.S. Peirce. In contrast to the simple dyadic model of signs, advocated by Saussure, Peirce's triadic model of the sign facilitates the incorporation of contextual determination into the account of linguistic communication by signs. Peirce's model claims that the *signans* (or *signifiant*) is related to the *signatum* (or *signifie*) in a way that evokes, concurrently, a third set of phenomena: interpretants. The role of the interpretant is, according to Granger, to serve as a 'commentary, a definition, a gloss' on the relation between *signans* and *signatum*. Granger relates this model to the interpretation of the signs *in situation*, and speaks of the meaning produced by this process as co-determined by an abstract structure—the *a priori* grammar of the language—and by the evocation of various experiential factors of the interactional situation, i.e. by *a posteriori* interpretants.[16] In this way, the semiotic theory of Peirce, adapted in part by Granger, matches the double 'emic' account proposed by the Jakobsonians. In both cases, a second set of criteria are postulated to account for the necessary relation of sign to situation.

It is also illuminating that the technical term which Jakobson most frequently appends, in parenthesis, to whichever expression is used to denote the 'focus' of the message, is *Einstellung*, a term used in the theory of problem solving. *Einstellung* in this context refers to 'a habitual procedure for dealing with repeatedly encountered problems of a similar type'.[17] In this light it may be seen that the problem to be solved is the communication of a message and that the habitual procedure available for doing so, according to Jakobson, involves the relation of the linguistic message to its interpretants, i.e. to one or more of the constitutive factors of the speech event.

[16]Granger 1968, p. 120.
[17]Bullock and Stallybrass 1977, p. 195.

Furthermore, there is a most revealing difference between this theory and Bally's notion of the dialectic of interaction. Bally felt that, in order to communicate thoughts, the language-user is always forced to subjugate the personal nature of those thoughts to the interpersonal conventions of language. In this way, the language-user can never say all that he wants to say, but only what the language will allow him to say. But this restriction is necessary, argued Bally, because without such conventions no communication at all would be possible. Nevertheless, Bally felt that a limited degree of personal expressivity can be communicated due to the incrustation of expressive values into *la langue*. In an important deviation from Bally, Jakobson does not adopt the position that certain signs have their own expressive qualities. Instead Jakobson argues that expressivity, like the other functions of language, is a question of the relation between the message and the situational context, i.e. a question of *parole*. Paradoxically, this is perhaps a more strictly Saussurian view, in spite of the fact that Bally, much more than Jakobson, was a devoted disciple of Saussure.

This difference may be seen in the following example: *Why don't you come see us sometime?* This can be taken, depending on the situation, in a number of ways. It could be seen, for instance, as an invitation, in which case Jakobson would say that it has a conative function. However, it could also be taken as a request for information (viz. why the addressee will not visit the addresser) or as a complaint: that is, with either a referential or emotive function. Bally's model is unable to account for the difference between these possible interpretations because the actual signs involved do not change from situation to situation. Hence any explanation based on finding expressivity in the signs *la langue* is restricted here to one, and only one, reading. This would seem to attribute greater explanatory power to Jakobson's account.

Jakobson acknowledges the polysemical nature of the linguistic utterance *ex situ*. By attributing values such as expressivity and literarity to *parole* (whereas Bally placed them in *la langue*) he is not forced to define these values in relation to individual signs taken, as it were, out of context. Instead his analysis focuses on whole utterances, studied in, and in relation to, contexts of occurence. The signs of the language are thus pictured not simply as empty of any expressive content, but essentially, as of infinite potential, capable of fulfilling a variety of tasks depending on the context of their use.

Yet, surprisingly, as far as the poetic function is concerned, Jakobson denies the role of the situation in determining this particular function of the message. Instead the fact that a message has a poetic function is determined solely by certain of its *linguistic* features. Thus the situational meaning of the poetic message, the message with what is called 'style' by the Jakobsonians, is not determined by any other factor of the speech event than the linguistic form of the message itself. The poetic message remains, in this sense ambiguous and autonomous, since no other factor of the speech event serves to reduce its limitless potential for meaning. Nonetheless, the poetic message is distinctive for other reasons.

We have already seen that the poetic function is defined as 'the set (*Einstellung*) toward the message as such, focus on the message for its own sake'. Within the context of our explanation of the phenomenological background of Jakobson's theory, it may be seen that this definition implies that the poetic message promotes its interpretation not in relation to a referent, nor to its addressee, but, specifically, to itself *as* a message. It focuses on its own constitutive linguistic structure. The word is seen not as a substitute for the referent but as indicating its own operability as a sign. Thus like Bally's soldier whose actions in war games have the function of referring to themselves, as examples of the correct actions in such a situation, the linguistic message with a poetic function calls attention to the way in which it functions as a linguistic sign; i.e. the interpretant of the poetic message is nothing but itself.

This function, by promoting the palpability of signs, deepens the fundamental dichotomy of signs and objects.[18]

'But why,' one might ask, 'is this any different from having no interpretant at all, from being interpreted *ex situ*?' For the answer to this question we will first have to turn to Jakobson's explanation of the empirical, linguistic criterion which distinguishes the poetic message.

The linguistic criterion of the poetic function

What is the empirical linguistic criterion of the poetic function? In particular, what is the indispensable feature inherent in any piece of poetry? To answer this question we must recall the two basic modes of arrangement used in verbal behaviour, *selection* and *combination*. . . . The selection is produced on the base of equivalence, simiarity and dissimilarity, synonymity and antonymity, while the combination, the build up of the sequence, is based on contiguity. *The poetic function projects the principle of equivalence from the axis of selection into the axis of combination.* Equivalence is promoted to the constitutive device of the sequence.[19]

This passage from the 'Linguistics and Poetics' article is probably the most famous and influential paragraph in modern stylistics, and the sentence 'The poetic function projects the principle of equivalence from the axis of selection into the axis of combination' is certainly the rallying cry for post-Bally structural stylistics. And yet, at first glance, it certainly could not be said to be self-explanatory. The conceptual background for this statement lies in the Saussurian notion of the paradigmatic and syntagmatic structures of language. This is a view

[18]Jakobson 1960, p. 356.
[19]Jakobson 1960, p. 358.

to which Jakobson subscribes, seeing it as a general organizing principle which underlies the structure of all language. Since it plays such a large role in the formulation of Jakobson's notion of the poetic function it will best serve our explanatory purposes here to investigage this perspective on the 'two-fold character of language'.

Jakobson's theory of the paradigmatic and syntagmatic axes of language structure is clearly and simply explained in Part 2 of *Fundamentals of Language*. This second part was written by Jakobson alone (the rest of the book was written with Morris Halle) and is entitled 'Two Aspects of Language and Two Types of Aphasic Disturbances'. In the second chapter he writes:

> Any linguistic sign involves two modes of arrangement:
> (1) Combination. Any sign is made up of constituent signs and/or occurs only in combination with other signs. This means that any linguistic unit at one and the same time serves as a context for simpler units and/or finds its own context in a more complex linguistic unit: combination and contexture are two faces of the same operation.
> (2) Selection. A selection between alternatives implies the possibility of substituting one for the other, equivalent to the former in one respect and different from it in another. Actually, selection and substitution are two faces of the same operation.[20]

This is a widely held theory of language structure, propounded also, in one form or another, by such differing linguists as Bloomfield, Martinet, Hjelmslev, and Chomsky. Saussure, in his *Cours de linguistique générale* maintained that 'in a language-state everything is based on relations' and that 'relations and differences between linguistic terms fall into two distinct groups'.[21] These two groups he describes as relations *in praesentia* which are equivalent to Jakobson's syntagmatic relations, and relations *in absentia,* or Jakobson's paradigmatic relations.

It is important that we pay particular attention to Jakobson's notion of paradigmatic structure since it is this structure's organizing principle of equivalence which is 'projected into the axis of combinations' that is, into the syntagmatic sequence of the message, to create the set toward the message, i.e. the poetic function. In other words, the structure that is superimposed on the message—the *surcodage* of the stylistic structure—is in fact of the same type as the paradigmatic structure. This superimposed structure, like the structure of the paradigmatic axis, is formulated 'on the base of equivalence, similarity and dissimilarity, synonymity and antonymity'. Thus, in general, the Jakobsonian approach sees the empirical criterion of the poetic function of a message as the

[20]Jakobson and Halle 1956, p. 60.
[21]Saussure 1978, p. 170.

repetition, (whether total or partial) of sounds, of meanings, of complete signs, of intonation patterns, and so on. In this way, in addition to the normal relations between units in the sequence, that is, relations based on *in praesentia* contiguity, there is incorporated into the structure of the sequence a supplementry set of relations, based on the criterion of code-determined equivalence. Another way of looking at this superposition of structure is to see the poetic message as self-focusing due to the positional association (e.g. by juxtaposition, by similar positioning in clauses, in stanzas, etc.) of linguistic features that are already associated *by convention* in the code. This superposition of conventional association onto positional association is called 'coupling' by S.R. Levin.

> In ordinary messages, we usually find no relation existing between two forms occurring at corresponding positions in the message . . . The important effect of coupling is to unite *in praesentia* terms that are otherwise united *in absentia*. . .[22]

Furthermore, the foundation, or relational principle, of all associations in the code is equivalence. However, two linguistic features may be conventionally related by equivalence for a variety of reasons, e.g. because they are both free variants in a particular context, because they mean the same, because they are semantic opposites (antonymy, in this way, is also based on equivalence), because they accent the same syllable, etc. Such relations of equivalence which are, in the non-poetic message, *in absentia,* become *in praesentia* in the poetic message. This is not hard to see in such an example as the last stanza of Poe's 'The Raven' which, as noted by Jakobson, contains a great deal of alliteration.[23]

> And the Raven, never flitting, still is sitting, *still* is sitting
> On the pallid bust of Pallas just above my chamber door;

The phonological equivalences of *flitting, sitting,* and *still* and of *pallid* and *pallas,* equivalences which themselves are not relevant to the determination of the linguistic meaning or referential function of the message, are here quite noticeable and attract attention to the linguistic constitution of the message.

Or, in the following lines of Hilaire Belloc, it may be seen that certain features of the message are relevant to two different aspects of communication:

> I shoot the hippopotamus
> With bullets made of platinum
> Because if I use leaden ones
> His hide is sure to flatten 'em.

[22]Levin 1962, p. 371.
[23]Jakobson 1960, p. 371.

Here both expressions, *platinum* and *flatten 'em*, are relevant to the meaning of the message. However, the similarity of their phonological structure makes no difference to the (conceptual or linguistic) meaning at all. Nevertheless, it *is* relevant to the poetic function of the poem. This meaningless phonological structure of equivalences is superimposed on the grammar of the sentence to give the lines a poetic function.

Moreover, according to the portion of linguistic theory common to Saussure and Jakobson, it is by way of its coded, *in absentia* relations that the meaning of a linguistic sign is determined. In other words, it is the sign's place within the structure of the code (or, *la langue*)—a structure that is made up of relations—that gives the linguistic sign its meaning *ex situ*. The phenomenological notion of the message's primary 'set toward' its grammar is in fact a 'set toward' the meaning-determining coded relations into which enter the signs constituting the message. Similarly, the poetic message exhibits a second 'set' toward those coded relations which are instantiated in the sequential structure of the message. This is the 'focus on the message as such'.

When these relations—ordinarily *in absentia*—appear *in praesentia* within the syntagmatic structure of the message, they provide two often analysed effects. The first effect is primarily formal while the second influences the possible meanings of the message. First of all, they reveal or foreground the message's own constitutive structure. That structure is determined by the set towards the *in absentia* relations of the grammar, and, in the poetic message, some of these relations are themselves revealed *in praesentia*. This is what was seen in the example from 'The Raven'. The Jakobsonian claims that because of this explicit presentation, in the sequence itself, of some code-determined relations between signs, the relations between other signs, ordinarily irrelevant, become more important in the poetic message. A little explicit similarity, in this sense, breeds more. It is not just the few obvious instances of alliteration, oxymoron, and metaphor that are foregrounded in the poem, but indeed all of the equivalences between signs: e.g. equivalence of gender, of tense, of part of speech, of distinctive-feature composition, etc. Any paradigmatic grammatical relation that a sign has with another sign acquires a potential relevance which it would not have in a non-poetic message. The poetic message becomes a hall of mirrors, with every sign reflecting its relation to other signs in the message, hence explicitly foregrounding its relationally-determined value in the code.

> In poetry one syllable is equalized with any other syllable of the same sequence; word stress is assumed to equal word stress, as unstress equals unstress; prosodic long is matched with long, short with short; word boundary equals word boundary, no boundary equals no boundary; syntactic pause equals syntactic pause, no pause equals no pause. Syllables are converted into units of measure and so are morae or stresses.[24]

[24]Jakobson 1960, p. 358.

In this way, the linguistic—rather than the pragmatic or communicational—nature of the message is more apparent in poetry. The poetic message is not taken so much as 'talking *about*'—whether about the referent, or the addresser, or the addressee—but instead as promoting the recognition of its constitution *as* a message, as this is determined by its set toward the grammatical conventions of the code. This aspect of the poetic message, which Bally referred to as the concentration on the means rather than on the ends of expression, is what the Jakobsonians take as the source of the opacity of poetic expression.

The nature of the poetic function is perhaps best explained by analogy. When a movie is made in which the cameras, cameramen, director, and so on, are all quite visible on the screen, the effect is to prevent the audience from seeing the movie's story as a real slice of life which they are just fortunate enough to see on film. Instead the awareness is continuously forced on the audience that the movie is both fictional and artificial; its constitution as a cinematic artifact is highlighted. Similarly in poetic language the reader is made to notice the language-dependent, semiotic construction of the message. He is thereby kept from paying attention only to the meaning of the message. (In the next chapter we will see that Riffaterre, among others, did not believe that a sequential structure of equivalences could affect the reader in this way.)

Secondly, there is a phenomenon known as 'parallelism'. The fact that meaning-determined relations of the code are instantiated in the message produces a 'hesitation' as to the meaningfulness of their role in the sequence. In this way those signs in the poetic message which are similar in form suggest a possible meaning-determining relation between them. This is what Paul Valery called 'hesitation between sound and sense',[25] reformulated by Jakobson as follows:

> Briefly, equivalence in sound, projected into the sequence as its constitutive principle, inevitably involves semantic equivalence, and on any linguistic level any constituent of such a sequence prompts one of the two correlative experiences which Hopkins neatly defines as 'comparison for likeness' sake' and 'comparison for unlikeness' sake'.[26]

The 'comparison for likeness' sake' and 'comparison for unlikeness' sake' constitute the principle of parellelism and as such exhibit the second 'set' by the message toward a factor of the speech event. However, in this case the factor is the message itself. As a result the meaning of the poetic message is not determined by the situation, as in the case of the message with a focus on either the referent, addresser, or addressee. Instead, it is determined entirely by the code: first, through the primary 'set toward' the grammar of the code, and secondly, through the 'set toward' the coded relations in the message itself. Hence the

[25]Jakobson 1960, p. 367.
[26]Jakobson 1960, pp. 368-9.

poetic message is ambiguous. Any formal relation between signs in the sequence is potentially meaningful, and no pragmatic focus on the situational context is present to resolve this ambiguity. The poetic message is not simply ambiguous in the manner of an utterance taken out of context. This would be the result of taking the example, *What a rotten day*, out of context. Is it an expression of disgust, or a description, or a hint, or a gloss? While, for the non-poetic message, the effect of contextualization is disambiguity, the ambiguity of the poetic message is on the contrary, *exaggerated*, because of the potentially significant relations between signs in the same sequence. Thus, Jakobson argues:

> Ambiguity is an intrinsic, inalienable character of any self-focused message, briefly a corollary of poetry.... The supremacy of the poetic function over referential function does not obliterate the reference but makes it ambiguous.... The repetitiveness effected by imparting the equivalence principle to the sequence makes reiterable not only the constituent sequences of the poetic message but the whole message as well. This capacity for reiteration whether immediate or delayed, this reification of the poetic message and its constituents, this conversion of a message into an enduring thing, indeed all this represents an inherent and effective property of poetry.[27]

Realism in stylistics

Finally, it is essential to note a fundamental presupposition in Jakobson's theory. The twofold structure of paradigm and syntagm is postulated not as a feature of linguistic analysis, but as an inherent characteristic of language itself. In other words, linguistic analysis is seen as describing a universal—the axes of language—from an epistemological perspective that is decidedly realist as opposed to nominalist. This is different, in some ways, from the American distributionalist's viewpoint. They also speak of paradigmatic and syntagmatic relations between units of language but their use of this framework is essentially for the purposes of classification, i.e. as a discovery procedure. But Jakobson attributes this framework to language itself and not to the linguist's descriptive model. It is one thing to say that we may describe the structure of a language by classifying features according to what we, as analysts, determine to be their substitution and combination possibilities. An entirely different ontological claim is presupposed by saying that these classes are part of the social object that is in the language. This is akin to the question of whether there really *are* class divisions in any given society, or whether analysts have invented them for theoretical and descriptive purposes, or to the question of whether 'redness' is a feature of the world, i.e. a characteristic possessed by red things, or merely a feature of our common-sensical classification of things in the world. Jakobson's realist ontological

[27]Jakobson 1960, p. 371.

stance in linguistics is underlined by the fact that his remarks on the twofold character of language appear in an article on aphasia in which he explains aphasic disorders, observable in the patient's behaviour, as stemming either from a 'similarity disorder' or a 'contiguity disorder'.[28] Such disorders could not be the product of the analyst's description.

In his book on Jakobson's theory of language, Holenstein compared the epistemological perspective of the natural scientist with that of Jakobsonian structuralism.

> A physicist has to establish agreement between two sets of data: the facts of nature and the system of the theory. A linguist is confronted with three data groups: the message or object language of the sender, the code of the sender, and the metalanguage or theory of the linguist.
>
> With the three fields of reference, code-message-metalanguage, structuralism propounds a synthesis of the logico-positivistic and phenomenological explanations. For the positivistic explanation, the criterion, in addition to observational adequacy (adjustment to the object) and consistency (absence of contradiction), is the greatest possible simplicity of explanatory principles. The additional criterion for phenomenology is its intuitive givenness. Structuralism aims at grasping a thing both from within and without through explanatory means that can be constructed as theoretical artifacts and at the same time disclosed as mental phenomena. The apprehension from within and without must be made to coincide.[29]

The structuralist stylistician accepts this position with a sigh of relief, for the Jakobsonian account of the poetic function relies on the commitment that the axes of similarity and contiguity are inherent to language and not just a figment of an imaginative descriptive apparatus. If they were only classificatory procedures, how could the stylistician speak of poetic language as an instance of 'the projection of the principle of equivalence from the axis of selection into the axis of combination'? Is a language capable of projecting a principle of descriptive classification? In other words, it is essential that the dual structure not be seen simply as a part of the linguist's description. Otherwise it would make no sense to speak of style as a superimposed structure, since that structure would have the dubious ontological status of a projected description.

We may now see the attraction of the Jakobsonian approach in relation to the epistemological problem presented in the beginning of this chapter, viz. the 'real' or 'nominal' constitution of a social object denoted by the terms 'style' or 'literarity'. The Jakobsonian argues not only that the style of a message is something concrete and observable—hence taking the 'realist' position—but that

[28]Jakobson and Halle 1956, part II.
[29]Holenstein 1976, pp. 59-60.

the study of style may be approached using the already established categories and distinctions available in linguistics, and specifically, a 'realist' linguistics as advocated by Jakobson. In this way the problems stylistics has with criteria and categorization—those problems which proved to be Bally's weakness—may conveniently be swept under the carpet of a confident, realist linguistics. This possibility is closely tied to the view that there is nothing 'new', or uniquely 'poetic' or 'stylistic', which is injected into an ordinary message in order to give it style. Instead, the same relations and distinctions of the code—already the subject matter of linguistics proper—are seen to be re-applied to the message in a slightly different way. Hence, the same method of analysis which is adequate for linguistics may itself be re-applied in stylistics analysis. In this sense, Jakobsonian stylistics may be seen—in a risky paronymy—as the projection of the analytical principles of linguistics (the study of the code) into the analysis of the message.

Still, Jakobson is not unique in this respect. Both Bally and Jakobson advocate linguistic reductionism as their approach to the study of style. Bally proposes to study expressive values in *la langue*. Jakobson argues that the source of literarity lies in a special application of the conventions of the code. Nevertheless, their approaches differ in a way that suggests the reason behind Jakobson's pre-eminence as the prophet of structure stylistics. In order to account for the expressive function of language in communication, Bally was led to postulate the existence of a separate class of values belonging to the signs of the language. To study these values a method had to be developed by which they could be separated from the non-expressive values—or, conceptual values—which are unlike expressive values in that they are determined solely by convention. Furthermore this method had to provide for the classification of expressive values into particular categories, e.g. recipient-design, 'effet d'évocation', 'effet naturel', etc. Bally hinted at the functional demarcation of these categories of values but then did not provide any functional criteria for their delimitation. As a result, the stylistician of the Bally school is left in a position where he senses that certain signs are more adequate for certain communicational purposes, but he has no apparatus by which to make such distinctions.

In comparison, the attraction of Jakobson's theory is, firstly, that it proceeds from a more detailed account of the functions of language and relates these to the analysis of particular messages *in situ*. Secondly it does not claim that individual signs have specific non-conceptual values that make each one more or less adaptable to specific functions. On the contrary, it argues that the same criteria and categories of linguistics, determined without reference to such fuzzy values as expressivity, affectivity, and recipient-design, are the only ones needed for the analysis of style. In this way, stylistics is not forced to burden language with values that seem fabricated, and so attract the linguist's contempt for unneeded psychologism. This advantage then, is that of the simplicity of the theoretical model. Jakobson proposes a simple theory that is adaptable to the explanation of a variety of phenomena. As Holenstein points out, Jakobson's theory is not only attractive for its realism—in postulating the mental reality of its theoretical constructs—but also for its simplicity, i.e. its ability to reduce the explanation of complex phenomena to a few fundamental principles: selection and combination.

In this sense, by adopting Jakobson's approach to their discipline, stylisticians acquire a ready-made, workable methodology: that of Jakobsonian or Prague School linguistics. For many years, structural stylistics had been at great pains to establish itself as a field, but without a clear, scientific notion even of what its object of investigation was, this proved an almost insurmountable task. From such mottos as *Le style—c'est l'homme meme* to Bally's problems in establishing categories of expressive effects, stylistics had been beset with impressionism. Considering the modern prejudice in academia for a scientific approach and positivism, such a problem could not fail to hinder the recognition of stylistics as a 'serious' discipline. The Jakobsonian movement in stylistics can, in this light, be seen as reacting against this lack of scientific rigour, by making stylistics part of the already developed, fashionable, and respectable science of linguistics.

4

Riffaterre and Affective Stylistics

Since the appearance of the 'Linguistics and Poetics' article in 1960 the loudest objections to Jakobson's theory have been voiced by a member of his own camp: the structuralist stylistician Michael Riffaterre. Still, although Riffaterre has taken issue with Jakobson over a variety of theoretical questions, the influence of the Jakobsonian method is quite apparent. Riffaterre does not deny this. Even in his most polemical articles, devoted solely to the criticism of Jakobson's theory—i.e. 'The Stylistic Function' and 'Describing Poetic Structures'[1]—Riffaterre makes quite clear not only where he and Jakobson diverge on theoretical issues but in what respects they agree. Like Bally, Riffaterre is greatly concerned with developing a method of stylistic analysis that is specifically suited to his theoretical perspective on the function of style in communication. And, like Jakobson, he believes that such a method should take advantage of the recent advances made in the science of linguistics. Riffaterre's approach in stylistics—as indeed his conception of the 'object' of this investigation—hinges on this crucial problem of the adaptation of method to theory.

The present chapter will have a double focus: to elucidate the theoretical background to Riffaterre's criticism of Jakobson and to evaluate the proposed remedies. It will be shown that Riffaterre's efforts result in an attempt to accommodate the subjective approach of Bally's theory within the objectivity of method advocated by Jakobson. After a preliminary review of Riffaterre's criticism of Jakobson, this criticism will be situated within a detailed analysis of the former's notion of the teleological function of style in communication, specifically, in written communication. Since, like Bally, Riffaterre argues that stylistics is concerned with the means of language's adaptation to communicational function, the analysis will be followed by an exposition of Riffaterre's model of the linguistic structure of style, and of the method proposed for the analysis of that structure. The latter half of the chapter will be devoted to an evaluation of this teleological model of stylistic structure and to an analysis of the adaptation of Jakobson's method to such a perspective.

---

[1]All four of the articles under discussion in this chapter have been published in both English and French editions, the latter in a collection of articles entitled *Essais de stylistique structurale*. This collection (1971) contains a great many corrections and additions, made by Riffaterre himself, to the earlier, English versions of the articles. Where no such adjustments have been made, references will be to the English versions, including, in addition to the two articles mentioned above, "Criteria for Style Analysis" and "Stylistic Context". Otherwise references will be to the text of the French edition. All translations are my own.

Criticism of Jakobson

An interesting illustration of Riffaterre's position is provided by his definition of the 'object' of stylistic investigations. Whereas Bally pictures stylistics as the study of expressivity in language, and Jakobsonians see it as the study of verbal art, Riffaterre proposes that these two studies are really one and the same; that is, the study of verbal art (or literary style) only investigates a more complex form of the same phenomenon: linguistic expressivity.

> Stylistics... studies the act of communication not as merely producing a verbal chain, but as bearing the imprint of the speaker's personality, and as compelling the addressee's attention. In short, it studies the ways of linguistic efficiency (expressiveness) in carrying a high load of information. The more complex techniques of expressiveness can be considered—with or without esthetic intentions on the author's part—as verbal art, and stylistics thus investigates literary style.[2]

This not only indicates the influence of Bally's thought on Riffaterre—modified as it was by the literary preoccupations of Cressot and Marouzeau—but also suggests the source of Riffaterre's differences with Jakobson. Essentially, Riffaterre accuses Jakobson's approach of irrelevance. Jakobson applies the categories and methodology of linguistics to the study of literary style. Riffaterre argues that such an approach is incapable of distinguishing in its analysis between stylistic phenomena and 'purely linguistic phenomena' because, in short, it pictures the act of communication as 'merely producing a verbal chain'. However, he claims that stylistic phenomena 'must have a specific character, since otherwise they could not be distinguished from linguistic facts'.[3] Because of the specific character of stylistic phenomena, a method of analysis that is purely linguistic will isolate only the linguistic functions of these phenomena 'without discerning which of their features makes them stylistic units as well'.[4] The Jakobsonian method reduces the analysis of style to linguistic analysis. The reason for this reduction lies in the definition of the poetic function as the projection of the principle of equivalence from the code into the message. However, Riffaterre argues that the style of a message, whether 'ordinary' or poetic, is more than just a structure of equivalences. Instead it has its own unique structure, different from that instantiated in the code. This structure has a teleological foundation in the function of style in communication. To study style simply as a structure of equivalences is to apply a method and a criterion which are adequate only for the analysis of the message *as* a verbal chain, as exhibiting a 'set toward' the gram-

[2]Riffaterre 1962, p. 316.
[3]Riffaterre 1959, p. 154.
[4]Riffaterre 1959, p. 154.

mar of the code. But the stylistic structure of a message has a distinct function in communicational interaction and this structure can only be discovered by developing both criteria and a method of analysis which are based on a prior elucidation of the role of style in communication. Stylistic analysis must therefore reflect this difference in orientation.

Riffaterre, in developing this point, argues that in order to take into account the communicational function of style, stylistics must formulate situational criteria for the delimitation of the stylistic phenomena in a message. These criteria should distinguish the stylistic from the linguistic function of a feature. Jakobson's method is accused of being too heavily based on the use of the code as criterion. For Riffaterre, because situational factors determine the function of style, they should also serve as criteria to differentiate, within the message, the stylistic from the purely linguistic. This step may be seen as a development of Bally's stylistic theory. However, it is a step that Bally never took.

In agreement with Riffaterre's criticism of Jakobson on this point, Jonathan Culler adds that equivalences within the sequential structure of the message are not unique to poetic or literary utterances. In his book *Structuralist Poetics* Culler makes this point both forcefully and playfully. He demonstrates that a Jakobsonian analysis of a passage of technical prose—indeed, a passage taken from Jakobson's own book: *Questions de poétique*—will uncover a great variety of sequential equivalences of the type that Jakobson attributes only to poetic language.[5] In this way, although the structure of equivalences, so central to Jakobson's notion of poetic language, might still be seen as a *necessary* condition of literariness, it can at least be proven not to be sufficient. An analogous criticism might be made of a linguistic theory which arbitrarily chose nazalization as a distinctive feature of speech without proving this claim by reference to the differential criterion of meaning. This objection would ask: but does the presence or absence of nazalization in any context affect the meaning of the message? Of course nazalization is frequent, but one cannot say that it is a relevant feature of speech unless it can be proved to have a communicational function (such as the differentiation of meaning in particular syntagmatic contexts). Exercises such as Culler's, or detailed criticism such as that made by Riffaterre of Jakobson and Levi-Strauss' analysis of 'Les chats',[6] show that, even if one accepts Jakobson's claim that the projection of the principle of equivalence into the message is an 'indispensable feature inherent in any piece of poetry',[7] this linguistic criterion is not the only or, as Riffaterre claims, not the *relevant* criterion. What Riffaterre does consider to be the relevant linguistic criterion of style derives from his notion of the specific function of style, which in turn depends on his theory of communicational interaction.

[5]Culler 1975, p. 63ff.
[6]Riffaterre 1966.
[7]Jakobson 1960, p. 358.

The communicational function of style.

Riffaterre argues that, because linguistic analysis is incapable of distinguishing between the stylistic and the 'purely linguistic' aspects of a message, 'our only solution is to observe and rearrange the data from a different angle'.[8] This different perspective is that of 'the whole act of communication' and specifically that of the addressee's role in communication. It is claimed, in effect, that the addressee (or reader for the specific case of literature) apprehends the linguistic message differently than do the analytic procedures of linguistics. Riffaterre appears to argue for something like Bally's notion of the dialectic between the subjective and the objective in communication, but whereas Bally emphasized the subjectivity of expression, Riffaterre focuses on the subjectivity of reception. Riffaterre is not so much concerned with how an individual might be able to encode his subjective experiences for the purpose of communication, but rather with how, as an addressee, he could decode such expression, i.e. with how communication might be achieved.

A purely linguistic analysis of the message will necessarily neglect the function of the message in the communicational interaction between two (or more) individuals. For if the interactional domain is taken into account the message must be seen not as an objective reality subject to scientific (linguistic) analysis, but as essentially a subjective reality, constituted by the perceptual faculties of addresser and addressee. In this way, Riffaterre argues, any analysis of the message should, in a sense, 'pass through' the perception of the message by the interactants; i.e. it must take as criterion of analysis the nature of the subjective perceptual analysis carried out by the interactants themselves.

In the later edition of his 'Criteria for Style Analysis' Riffaterre is quite explicit in claiming that, as far as stylistics is concerned, the message must be seen not as an objective reality but as an impression subjectively constructed in the mind of the addressee.

> ...the object of the analysis of style is the illusion that the text creates in the mind of the reader.[9]

In other words, the linguistic message is seen as relating not only to the structure of the language but also to a factor of the communication situation viz. the addressee. (This is not to say that Riffaterre denies the notion, so central to Jakobsonian thought, of the 'set toward the message'. More will be said about this later.) Thus, a consideration of how the message is perceived by the addressee, that is, of what Riffaterre calls the 'illusion' that the message produces in the mind, is a necessary prerequisite to the formulation of a correct theory of the

[8]Riffaterre 1966, p. 214.
[9]Riffaterre 1971, p. 49.

nature and function of style. With this argument, Riffaterre leads the functional perspective in stylistics, the perspective initiated by Bally and advanced by Jakobson, further into the domain of the psychological. This trend, affective stylistics, dominates stylistics for the next twenty years.

Literary style, according to Riffaterre, arises out of the author's preoccupation with surmounting the difficulties encountered in the communication of his message to the reader. In spoken communication, the speaker has at his disposal such communicational aids as eye-contact, intonation, gesture etc. Furthermore, many such situations will be two-party administered. The speaker may repeat himself if he suspects his interlocutor is not following, or he may directly ask his interlocutor if he understands. A variety of clues are available by which he may determine, to a sufficient degree of satisfaction, whether the 'illusion' that his message creates in the hearer's mind is as intended. This 'illusion', if the complex phenomenon of understanding may be spoken of as such, is, in many ways, negotiable. However, in written communication 'the writer has to do much more to get his message across'.[10] The interactants are, for one thing, separated by space and time. Because of this situation the writer is unable to avail himself of conversational tools to ensure, to his own satisfaction, that his message is being subjectively perceived and interpreted according to his intentions. In other words, the increased distance between addresser and addressee renders the interactional dialectic of communication even more acute. Furthermore, Riffaterre insists, the goals of literary communication are different from 'mere communication'.[11] There are the complexities of expressive, affective, and esthetic connotations to be transmitted. Both because of these increased demands and because of the limitations imposed by writing, the author is forced to turn to other methods to ensure the reception of his intended message.

Riffaterre claims that the primary obstacle that the writer must surmount, in order to communicate all that he intends, is what he calls 'minimal decoding' by the reader.

> The meaning of a message can be received with minimal decoding. More is required if the writer wants to force upon his reader's attention certain formal features to which he attaches special importance (e.g. aesthetic intent). But what permits minimal decoding is that it is possible with variable accuracy to predict, from part of a sequence, the features which follow.[12]

Taking as his source experiments carried out within the paradigm of the behaviourist theory of information, Riffaterre points out that reading, like perception of a spoken utterance, is often an elliptical process.

[10]Riffaterre 1959, p. 157.
[11]Riffaterre 1959, p. 157.
[12]Riffaterre 1960, p. 207.

Because the probability of occurrence in the written chain varies for different features 'it is possible, from a part of the sequence, to predict with greater or lesser accuracy the succeeding features.[13]

In this way the reader can get the gist of a written utterance by focusing on only a few of its components.

But as the writer of literature attaches great importance to a correct reading of his message he must employ a specific verbal strategy to prevent such a 'minimal decoding' process by the reader. For Riffaterre, this is *the* function of style. Agreeing with Jakobson that a 'focus on the message as such' characterizes the poetic message, Riffaterre argues that this may only be achieved if the writer succeeds in overcoming the 'natural behaviour' of the reader by making him pay close attention to the message. Such an emphasis on the message can only be accomplished, Riffaterre claims, by a verbal strategy based on surprise. The writer must encode in his message—at the points where he deems it most important—unpredictable linguistic elements. Since it is the high predictability of the written message which permits 'minimal decoding' the only strategy to counteract this natural habit of readers is to make certain elements of the message unpredictable. Such a device will arrest his normal, elliptical reading and cause him to pay closer attention to the message.

If (the author) wants to be sure that (his intentions regarding the interpretation of the message) are respected, he will have to control the decoding by encoding, at the points he deems important along the written chain, features that will be inescapable no matter how perfunctory the reception. And since predictability is what makes elliptic decoding sufficient for the reader, *inescapable elements will have to be unpredictable.*[14]

Since predictability will result in minimal decoding or elliptical reading, the writer is said to have only one recourse open to him; in order to ensure the communication of his message he must 'prevent the reader from inferring or predicting any important feature'. Riffaterre speaks of this strategy as 'limiting the freedom of perception in the process of decoding'.[15] In other words, if the author wants the reader to pay more than minimal attention to the message, the former will have to tailor his message in a way that responds appropriately by counteracting the natural behaviour of the reader. Thus, Riffaterre pictures the writer as adapting his message to a set of requirements imposed by the situation or speech event. In contrast to the position held by Bally that a language itself reflects requirements imposed upon it by communication, Riffaterre's position is that it is

[13]Riffaterre 1959, p. 158.
[14]Riffaterre 1959, p. 158.
[15]Riffaterre 1959, p. 159.

the writer who adapts his message to those requirements. And he pictures the primary requirement to be the focusing of the reader's attention. Like Bally again, Riffaterre sees this adaptation of the message to the needs of communication as constituting that message's expressivity.

> A control of the decoding is just what differentiates expressivity from ordinary writing.[16]

On the other hand, Jakobson's theory does not view the poetic message as adapted to the requirements of communication. Instead, the projection of equivalence into the message is seen as, in a sense, detaching it from the situation, rendering it ambiguous and non-pragmatic.

Consequently, it may be seen that although both Jakobson and Riffaterre claim that literarity (or style) is characterized by a 'focus on the message as such', Riffaterre goes further in attempting to explain both how this might be carried out, and to what purpose. This amounts to replacing the poetic message as object of investigation, back within, and as a functioning part of, the communicational act. For Riffaterre's argument reveals what appears to be a fundamental oversight in the Jakobsonian theory; Jakobson does not explain how the focus of the message on itself is communicated to the addressee. Riffaterre insists, in effect, that no message is *ex situ*; there is always at least the vital interaction between message and addressee[17] which results in the message's subjective construction as a perceptual object. If the message is to focus on itself as such—or indeed on any of the factors of the speech event—this focus must itself be communicated to the addressee. The question posed to Jakobson is, in short: how does the message get the reader to know what the focus is? How does it limit his freedom of perception so that he will see the message as focusing on itself? Riffaterre feels that, because of the nature of the reading process, the only possible answer is that it does so by the unpredictability of certain of its features. In this way, unpredictability constitutes a second channel of contact between the message and the reader, the first being the message's relation to the code of the language, common to both speaker and hearer. The writer's manipulation of this second, albeit dependent, channel of contact between message and addressee may be seen to constitute his individual style of writing. Because of the nature of this mechanism only the reader, and not linguistic analysis alone, can identify the stylistic elements of a message.

Riffaterre pictures this special encoding strategy as the writer's response to his preoccupation with having his message interpreted in the way that he intends, including aesthetic or expressive connotations.

---

[16]Rifaterre 1959, p. 159.
[17]Riffaterre 1966, p. 214.

The author's consciousness is his preoccupation with *the way he wants his message to be decoded,* so that not only its meaning but his attitude towards it is conveyed to the reader, and the reader is forced to understand, naturally, but also to share the author's view of what is or is not important in his message.[18]

By restricting the addressee's reading of the message, the writer, in effect, is able to impose his own second 'set' upon the message—as the first is itself imposed by the grammar of the language. This keeps the reader from setting the message within his own (idiosyncratic) interpretational context, and thus extends the writer's control over the act of communication. Restricted himself by the lack of contact with the reader, the writer is thus provided with a strategy to surpass this barrier so that his influence in the communicational interaction is not dangerously reduced. This would not be possible if the reader were allowed to skim over the message seeking only to 'get the gist' of its meaning.

It is interesting that Riffaterre's characterization of the reading process takes into account only the polar opposition of minimal and maximal decoding. This is primarily due to his allegiance to behaviourist information-theory. Riffaterre refers to the cline or continuum between these two poles of reading as that of 'intensity of reception'.[19] In the last chapter we noted that the structure of a language may be seen as a perceptual 'grid' against which the message is placed in order to determine its grammar. Similarly, Riffaterre views the reading process as structured in such a way that it forces a second perceptual 'grid' on the message. Depending on the message's adaptation to this 'grid' the reader will either 'minimally' or 'maximally' decode. The message's adaptation to this 'grid' also is seen as unidimensional, consisting of the binary opposition of marked versus unmarked, i.e. the unpredictability versus predictability of linguistic features. Riffaterre seems to feel that the interaction of these two sets of binary oppositions—minimal versus maximal decoding and predictability versus unpredictability—represents the only way in which the structure of the message may effect the structure of the reading process. This must be open to question. Could there not be other factors involved in the 'natural behaviour of the reader' which are not so easily characterized according to the cline of reading intensity? Is it not possible that other qualities of linguistic features, besides their degree of predictability, might have an effect on the reading process? Riffaterre's behaviourist theory of the function of the language in communication may be too limited by the undimensionality of its models. Riffaterre's answers to these theoretical questions lie in his proposals for a method of stylistic analysis.

Style, according to Riffaterre, is encoded into a message by the writer in response to certain requirements of communication, specifically, literary com-

---

[18]Riffaterre 1959, pp. 157-8.
[19]Riffaterre 1959, p. 158.

munication. This strategy renders certain elements of the message unpredictable so that the reader's attention will be drawn to them. In contrast to the stylistic theories advocated by Bally, Cressot, and Marouzeau, Riffaterre claims that there are no linguistic features that are *ipso facto* unpredictable. Instead the predictability or unpredictability of a particular feature depends entirely on the context of its use. Hence, its expressive value is not due to a decontextualized position in *la langue*, but, rather, due to its context in *la parole*. The disagreement here with Bally is evident. A linguistic feature is seen by Riffaterre to be unpredictable only if it occurs in a linguistic context with which it contrasts. In this way the locution *obscure clarté* is a stylistic device because of the appearance of the term *clarté* in the context *obscure—*. Of the terms which make up this oxymoron Riffaterre says that 'as constituents of a single structure, they form the least probable unit; *clarté* stands in contrast with the context *obscure; obscure clarté* is the stylistic device apprehensible as a unit'.[20] Therefore, the stylistic structure of a message is seen not just as a series of unpredictable linguistic features, but as composed of units or stylistic devices, that is, as a structure of individual features which are rendered unpredictable by one, or a pattern of more than one, contextual features. Contrast within context, the whole forms a stylistic unit which is only unpredictable due to the juxtaposition of the two parts.

The difference with the Jakobsonian notion of a structure of equivalences is quite clear. Riffaterre does say that equivalences play a role in the style of a message, but only if an unpredictable element appears which renders that pattern perceptible. Without this opposition to an unpredictable element the pattern is said to go unnoticed because of the natural behaviour of the reader. Thus, serving no communicational function, it cannot be considered part of the style of the message.

> Since stylistic intensification results from the insertion of an unexpected element into a pattern, it supposes an effect of rupture which modifies the context. . . . The stylistic context is a linguistic *pattern suddenly broken by an element which was unpredictable*, and the contrast resulting from this interference is the stylistic stimulus.[21]

So neither the unpredictability (or abnormality) of a particular expression nor the equivalence of a set of features is seen as determined by the code *as far as the reader's perception of them is concerned*. Both are determined, instead, by their clash within the sequence, one serving as a contrastive feature, the other as the context which both determines and is determined by the contrastive feature. The critic might wonder how such a peculiarly self-supporting system could be said to exist without some ground in values attributed to it by the code. The answer

[20]Riffaterre 1960, p. 210.
[21]Riffaterre 1959, p. 171.

that Riffaterre gives to this question perfectly underlines his deviation from both Bally and Jakobson: the fact that stylistic context and contrast clash and at the same time mutually determine one another stems not from the organization of the code, but from the perceptual structure of the reading process. Stylistic structure results from the interaction of the linguistic structure of the message and the perceptual structure of the reading process. In this way the reader's perception plays a large role in the determination of stylistic structure. But what kind of method could possibly permit the analyst to study such a structure?

Detecting the stylistic device: no smoke without fire

> This interdependence between the stylistic device and its perception is, in short, so central to the problem that it seems to me we may use this perception to locate stylistic data in the literary discourse. Unfortunately taste changes and each reader has his prejudices. Our problem is to transform a fundamentally subjective reaction to style into an objective analytical tool, to find the constant (encoded potentialities) beneath the variety of judgements, in short to transform value judgements into judgements of existence. The way to do it is, I believe, simply to disregard totally the content of the value judgement and to treat the judgement *as a signal only.*[22]

This quotation outlines the general principle beneath what Riffaterre calls his 'no smoke without fire' axiom. The problem for which it is formulated as a solution is the following: how may one deal with the phenomenon of subjectivity— which, after all, determines what is and what is not a stylistic device—by an objective method of analysis? A crucial point here is that Riffaterre believes that an objective analysis of style is indeed possible. He does not adopt the viewpoint held by some literary theorists that, because style is a phenomenon heavily tinged by subjectivity, the only appropriate investigative procedure should also be subjective since a quasi-objective procedure would *ipso facto* be a falsification. This is rejected as a needless pessimism which can only lead to the impressionism of Bally's expressive categories or to the categories of traditional literary criticism. And yet, Riffaterre warns against taking stylistics too far the other way, by incorporating it into a supposedly 'objective' linguistic analysis.

Instead he proposes a synthesis which consists in taking as raw data the subjective responses of readers to particular messages but treating those responses only as signals that those features to which they respond are stylistic devices. From that point onward linguistic analysis, guided by the knowledge of the perceptual processes of the reader, may continue the investigation. Furthermore, an advantage of such an approach is said to be that it takes into account that although 'the

[22]Riffaterre 1959, p. 162.

receiver's behaviour may be subjective and variable,...it has an objective in-variable cause.'[23] In this way the method proposed is able to admit that a reader's judgements regarding the style of a text may depend on his aesthetic taste, his literary prejudices, his schooling (including perhaps even which schools and which teachers influenced him), and on a variety of other influences which Rif-faterre groups under the heading 'value judgements'. But he insists that no mat-ter what the nature of these responses, they all must stem from the same linguistic sources, or, to use the behaviourist terminology employed by Rif-faterre, from the same 'stimuli'.

> Stripped of its formulation in terms of value, the secondary response becomes an objective criterion for the existence of its stylistic stimulus.[24]

It follows that it might at last be possible to construct a method of stylistic analysis which grounds its criterion of identification in the function of language in communication.

To this end, Riffaterre created a methodological device which he later came to call the *archilecteur*. Essentially the sum of the reactions to a text by a group of in-formants—including critics, translators, pundits, and poets alike—the *ar-chilecteur* serves the function of sorting out the stylistic features of a message from the features with no such function.

> Instead of starting with an arbitrary, culture-conditioned, common-sense segmentation of the text, or with an irrelevant (e.g. linguistic) one, the analyst is enabled to delimit the elements by which the author curbed the decoder's freedom (shallow reading, etc.) and increased the probability of perception.[25]

As such the *archilecteur* is a heuristic device or discovery procedure which, once having accomplished its task of locating the stylistic stimuli in a text, is then deemed to have exhausted its usefulness. The *archilecteur* is used only to locate the stylistic devices in a text; linguistic analysis has the task of explaining the structure of those devices. With this tool the analyst may use a variety of previous readings of his text—disregarding the criticism or 'value judgements' which they contain—and treat them, insofar as they are specific (i.e. focusing on particular points in text) as responses to encoded stylistic stimuli. Their responses thus serve as evidence of the existence of stylistic stimuli, but not as comments on the nature of those stimuli. In this way the analyst may 'disregard the reader's criticism as criticism, (and) observe it as behaviour'.[26] Thus the equation is

[23]Riffaterre 1959, p. 162.
[24]Riffaterre 1959, p. 163.
[25]Riffaterre 1959, pp. 165-6.
[26]Riffaterre 1959, p. 163.

established: if the reader's behaviour is 'unnatural'—i.e. his reception is intensified at certain points in the text—then there must be an unpredictable linguistic feature which provoked this behaviour: no smoke without fire.

This treatment of criticism not as criticism but as an indication of a particular type of behaviour (i.e. maximal decoding) raises a puzzling question for affective stylistics: is it feasible to disconnect response and stimulus? It is Riffaterre's opinion that reading proceeds according to two steps of development: first, the reader's attention is drawn by the form of the message, and then this perception is rationalized and interpreted according to the esthetic or other prejudices of the reader. It is, however, possible to object to this behaviourist argument and claim that a linguistic feature is itself only perceived as a stimulus due to the prejudices which are used to rationalize that perception. Riffaterre, in effect, claims that the perception of stylistic devices has only its own linguistic causes (viz. contrast within context) and that the nature of the value judgement has other causes (i.e. the prejudicial rationalizations). But the objection is that the nature of these prejudices might determine what is and what is not to count as a stimulus; i.e. the fact that 'x' is perceived as a stylistic device has some of the same causes as the rationalization of the response. This point of view recognizes the influence of 'cognitive predisposition' in perception and the role of 'looking for' in seeing. As a member of the 'New Look' school of perception-analysis Jerome Bruner argues that:

> Stimuli...do not act upon an indifferent organism.... The organism in perception is in one way or another in a state of expectancy about the environment. It is a truism worth repeating that the perceptual effect of a stimulus is necessarily dependent upon the set or expectancy of the organism.[27]

But, as we have already seen, not only does Riffaterre's behaviourism reduce the phenomenon of linguistic unpredictability to the binary opposition of contrast within context, it also reduces the problematic and complex domain of 'the reader's natural behaviour' to the invariant, unidimensional cline of reception intensity. In this way, what some psychologists call the 'biased nature of perceptual recognition' is reduced to the binary opposition of minimal versus maximal decoding.

Of course, it is by virtue of these reductions that Riffaterre is able to explain the function of stylistic structure in terms of the reading process and, vice versa, the structure of reading in terms of the unpredictability of style. The simplicity of this teleological theory of style depends on the notion of the parallel unidimensionalities of reading and unpredictability. Furthermore—and this is the main

[27]Bruner 1974, p. 68.

advantage of the theory's adaptability to scientific method—this simplicity permits the separation of stimulus from response. Due to the parallel unidimensionalities of reading and unpredictability, *intensification of response can be seen as having only one cause.* In addition, unpredictability may be seen as having one invariant effect: intensification of response. Any other factors of the reader's behaviour or of message structure are ignored (or reduced) so that this equation may be established. In this way, a theory based on subjectivity of response may be adapted to a method for the analysis of objective stimuli.

As an illustration of the objection raised to this separation of stimulus from response, one might consider the following archetypical cartoon of the duck-rabbit, taken from part II of Wittgenstein's *Philosophical Investigations* (paragraph 11).

Is the above a picture of a duck or a rabbit? In a sense, it is both but it could not be, for us, e.g. a rabbit if we had never seen one. We rely on our past experiences of having seen ducks, rabbits, pictures of ducks, and pictures of rabbits in order to perceive the above ink-marks as two different pictures. Thus, for us, what that stimulus is depends on our prior conditioning. Similarly, when I see the picture as a rabbit, the two 'fingers' on the left are seen as ears; when I see it as a duck, they form the beak. However, I cannot see them as lifting-forks because I cannot see the whole picture as a fork-lift truck. Nor, more importantly, can I see the whole picture as a rabbit, but the fingers as a beak. This would seem to indicate that our perception of one thing (e.g. the beak-ears) is sometimes determined by our perception of another thing (the duck-rabbit). In this sense an analysis of the stimulus of the beak-ears would be insufficient if it did not take into account whether I see them as a beak, as ears, as lifting forks, or as all three. For what they are for me is subjectively determined. But to take such aspects of perception into account would necessarily involve the analyst in extending his limits as to what may count as a condition or stimulus or response.

Related to Riffaterre's stance on this question is his belief that the stylistic function (his name for Jakobson's 'poetic function') is much more influential in the use of language than Jakobson had imagined. Arguing that while the other five functions all have in common their orientation to a point outside the message (referent, addresser, addressee, contact, or code,) the stylistic function 'is the only one centered on the message'.

> It seems therefore more satisfactory to say that communication is given structure by the five directional functions, and that its intensity (from expressiveness to verbal art) is regulated by the stylistic function.[28]

Riffaterre points out that both the emotive and conative functions, for example, work by drawing the attention of the reader to certain features of the message. This is accomplished by means of the message's stylistic function. That is, it is the message's structure of unpredictability within context that seems to focus the message on the addresser or addressee. Similarly, this 'regulatory' effect of the stylistic function is extended to the other functions of the message as well. For instance, 'even though a message may be ideally oriented towards the objective referent, its cognitive or denotative effectiveness depends on the effect of the sign on the addressee. . . .'[29]

In other words, Riffaterre seems to see the stylistic function as the 'workhorse' of the message's function in communication. Whatever other function a message may have will depend on its stylistic function. For it is this function's linguistic structure, based on unpredictability, that draws the addressee's attention to those features of the message which indicate its 'directional' function. Otherwise, the 'directional' function would not be communicated to the reader since he would only be minimally decoding. Riffaterre supports this claim by pointing out that 'the message and the addressee. . . are the only factors involved in (literary) communication whose presence is necessary'.[30] Thus the indication of a message's focus must be based on the interaction of these two factors. In this way, Riffaterre reduces the source of the communicational function of a message to its style, much as Bally had reduced expressivity in communication to the expressive values encoded in the signs of *la langue*. For Riffaterre, the communicational function of a message depends on the reader's response, and all such responses may be reduced to the perception of an unpredictable stimulus.

Furthermore, Riffaterre admits the subjective validity of Bally's 'expressive values' but attributes them to a misguided 'atomism' on the part of the reader who identifies his response with the linguistic stimulus that produced it. Riffaterre claims that this assumption by the reader—an assumption which is reproduced in Bally's theory of the expressive value of signs—involves two fundamental errors. First, the reader takes his own response as 'belonging to' the stimulus, assuming thereby that everyone will have the same response to that stimulus. This belief leads to the *langue* theory of expressive values in which it is

[28]Riffaterre 1962, p. 321.
[29]Riffaterre 1962, p. 321.
[30]Riffaterre 1966, p. 326.

assumed that each stimulus-expression has a set, inter-subjective response-content and that the relation between expression and content is a convention of the language. However, the nature of the response, argues Riffaterre, is determined not by the language but by other influences—e.g. culture, literary experiences, etc.—all unique to the individual. Bally's error is, in essence, taking the 'content' of the response (i.e. the value judgement) to be in a one-to-one relation with the stimulus expression, whereas Riffaterre points out that the objective relation is really between the stimulus and the mere existence of a response, of no matter what content.

The second common mistake which is incorporated into Bally's theory concerns the localization of the stimulus. The reader thinks that a particular linguistic feature caused his response, whereas it is the contrast between feature and context which, as a whole, provided the stimulus. 'The group as a whole (context plus contrast) forms the stylistic device'.[31] Bally's method, in effect, idealizes such a common response and treats individual expressions as possessing their own stylistic values; whereas it is only complete structures—contrast within context—which actualize such values. Even then, these values are not encoded in *la langue* but depend on the reader's culturally conditioned response to particular occurrences of those structures. Riffaterre says that the emphasis on discrete signs, which is a result of their unpredictability, monopolizes attention and creates in the mind of the reader what Riffaterre calls a 'paradigmatic memory'.

> Addressees react to a given word by isolating it from its context and comparing it mentally to a set of synonyms (e.g. *fugitivite de l'eau* will be compared to the more predictable *eau fuyante*).[32]

This 'paradigmatic memory' exactly represents the phenomenon that Bally proposed to exploit in order to determine the expressive value of a sign. Each sign was to be compared to its synonyms in order that its expressive value might be revealed. Bally argued that, in effect, this 'paradigmatic memory' is as real as any other knowledge of the code, and that it plays a large role in determining the stylistic effect of a sign in use. For Riffaterre, however, such a 'paradigmatic memory' is merely an illusion created from the effect of the reader's repeated encounters with signs in contexts when they are unpredictable. The proof of this, Riffaterre claims, is that these signs can easily be placed in contexts where no contrast arises and hence no stylistic effect. While this may be true, one might wonder, if Riffaterre's professed aim is to study the 'illusion' created in the mind of the reader why does this method systematically disregard such illusions?

---

[31]Riffaterre 1960, p. 209.
[32]Riffaterre 1962, p. 319.

No fire without smoke

So central is this notion of contrast within context to Riffaterre's methodology that he even suggests that the device of the *archilecteur* may be discarded 'at an advanced stage of analysis' and replaced by the 'determination of the minimal conditions for the perception of contrast in context'.[33] In other words, after much experience with the study of the reader's perception of stylistic devices, the stylistician should be able to determine on his own for any text which features would be perceptible. These features would always be part of a structure of contrast in context. In this way Riffaterre can be seen to modify his theoretical axiom—'No smoke without fire'—reversing it to the axiom guiding his method: 'No fire without smoke'. That the latter is not logically deducible from the former does not effect the practicality of its use for the linguistic analysis of style.

This is where Riffaterre's method of analysis more clearly resembles the method advocated by Jakobsonian structuralists. Simplistically, one may envisage the Jakobsonian examining a text for all of the equivalences between features that he can find, whereas the Riffaterrian will examine the same text looking only for patterns of equivalent features which are brought into contrast with another feature in the text. Such might seem to be the only difference that Riffaterre's emphasis on the reader's threshold of perception has created between his method and Jakobson's. But then, as their protracted debate over the poetic structure of Baudelaire's 'Les Chats' would attest, this can be a very crucial difference.[34]

Thus it would seem that the source of Riffaterre's difference with Jakobson is the former's respect for the subjective validity of the psychologism of Bally. Jakobson's linguistic-based analysis is, in effect, so 'objective' that it does not have the explanatory power of Bally's more intuitive approach. Affective Stylistics, as a method, Riffaterre might argue, must be scientific, taking full advantage of the recent gains made in linguistics. After all 'stylistic facts can be apprehended only in language, since that is their vehicle'.[35] But style as phenomenon and as object of investigation relies on its subjective constitution by the reader *reading*. In a sense, this phenomenon does not exist under the microscope of linguistic analysis but lies only in the eye of the beholder. The strength of Bally's efforts is that they elucidate how the phenomenon is seen by the reader, or at least by some readers, even though this may be a mere illusion. Riffaterre accepts this (. . . 'the object of the analysis of style is the illusion that the text creates in, the mind of the reader'[36]). But he feels that this illusion can only have been caused by certain linguistic facts about the message that is being

[33]Riffaterre 1971, p. 47.
[34]cf. Jakobson and Levi-Strauss 1962, Riffaterre 1966, and Jakobson 1973.
[35]Riffaterre 1959, p. 154.
[36]Riffaterre 1971, p. 49.

perceived. Language must 'give' us what we 'get' in communication. From where else could this illusion come?

> Obviously this illusion is not pure imagination or pure fantasy. It is conditioned by the structures in the text...[37]

In this way the linguistic analysis of Jakobson can be adapted to account for the subjective, yet non-scientific results of Bally's method. Bally's categories of expressive values can be explained—if not retained—by a linguistic analysis which takes into account the reader's role in communication. By a projection of the subjective response on to the objective reality of the text, Riffaterre arrives at a method by which such a response might be explained with purely linguistic methods of analysis.

Riffaterre supports his own version of stylistic structure on the grounds that it explains *how* a message could serve a functional purpose in communication, whereas Jakobson's notion of poetic structure seems to be chosen *ad hoc*. But Riffaterre is only able to provide this explanation by making two question-begging assumptions: first, that the occurrence of a response can only be due to a stimulus encoded in the text; and, second, that only a certain type of message structure can provide that stimulus. The Jakobsonian accused of an *ad hoc* determination of poetic structure might use as a rebuttal Riffaterre's *ad hoc* determination of how a message functions in communication.

The difference between Bally and Jakobson, as well as the synthesis realized by Riffaterre, can be seen in terms of their respective metalanguages. In order to explain certain phenomena which he felt to be different from ordinary, cognitive linguistic phenomena, Bally invented a language of description which consisted of categories and terms (e.g. 'natural effect', 'evocative effect') whose sole purpose was to name these subjectively perceived phenomena of style. Riffaterre admits the importance if not the objective validity of such terms.

> Their existence alone would suffice to justify a separate linguistics of the decoder, because the metalinguistic superstructure they constitute differs notably from the objective reality of the utterances.[38]

Jakobsonian stylistics, on the other hand, reacts against the subjective basis of Bally's metalanguage and instead chooses the already formulated and, in a sense, pre-tested 'realistic' metalanguage of modern linguistics. This language, as we saw in the last chapter, at least is based on categories which seem to be objectively identifiable and verifiable. Their validity, unlike Bally's categories, seems already to be assured from the sources other than the phenomenon they are meant to explain. In this lies both Riffaterre's agreement and disagreement with the metalanguage. Speaking of the description of poetry, he says,

[37]Riffaterre 1971, p. 49.
[38]Riffaterre 1962, p. 320.

R. Jakobson chose grammatical units to make this exegesis and many others because grammar is the natural geometry of language which superimposes abstract, relational systems upon the concrete, lexical material: hence grammar furnishes the analyst with ready-made structural units.[39]

Riffaterre's method of analysis advocates the use of such 'ready-made structural units' for the explanation of the structure of stylistic stimuli. However, he argues that they should be used only for the explanation of those stimuli that have already been singled out (or potentially could be) as stylistic by the subjective response of a set of readers. For it is this response (whether actual or potential) which, like Bally's notion of expressivity, indicates the subject matter of stylistic analysis. This sorting is essential for 'No grammatical analysis of a poem can give us any more than the grammar of the poem'.[40]

So, in effect, Riffaterre advocates a method of description which is based on the synthesis of two presupposed certainties: the subjective response of the reader and the objective, 'ready-made structural units' of linguistic analysis. Bally's intuitions are to be explained with Jakobson's terms. The wedding of two antithetical perspectives of subjectivity and objectivity is what may seem to account for both the intriguing ingenuity of Riffaterre's theory and the troubling *ad hoc* dependence of his method on the severely restricted notions of the 'natural behaviour of the reader' and unpredictability. These two notions form two bulkheads, each extending part of the way across this antithetical gap—one from the bank of the role of subjectivity in communication, the other from that of the objective arrangement of linguistic forms. Perched between these two is the bridge of Affective Stylistics.

In their book *Linguistique et poétique*, D. Delas and J. Filliolet warn about the instability of such a structure:

> ...it is difficult to combine the sum of signals that is the *archilecteur* with the minimal conditions of perceptability... This tempting equilibrium, between analytic and synthetic perspectives, is unstable by nature: an analysis cannot be simultaneously inductive and deductive.[41]

They go on to say that, as Riffaterre has himself suggested, the subjective criterion of the *archilecteur* tends in actual analysis, (including Riffaterre's) to be subsumed into the more objective criterion of contrastive elements within context. Presumably this would be acceptable in affective stylistics if it were possible to prove that, indeed, readers *never* notice anything but instances of contrast within context and, also, that they indeed notice *every* such instance.

[39]Riffaterre 1966, p. 213.
[40]Riffaterre 1966, p. 213.
[41]Delas and Filliolet 1973, p. 35.

This proof is not only lacking but Riffaterre seems to regard it as irrelevant. In his 'Criteria for Style Analysis' paper, Riffaterre emphasizes the priority of the criterion of contrast-within-context over that of the *archilecteur's* response.

> ...if there is no contextual contrast at the point where the (*archilecteur's*) reaction indicates the probable presence of a stylistic stimulus..., then we can assume that there was on the part of the (*archilecteur*) an over response to the text or an error by addition. In that case we may safely dismiss the initial clue.[42]

In other words, the surprising statement here made is that the *archilecteur's* response is of secondary importance in the identification of stylistic stimuli. Of primary importance is the presence in the message of the linguistic structure of contextual contrast. In this sense, objective linguistic data, and therefore linguistic analysis, takes precedence over the subjective data of response. It seems to be admitted here that, in fact, readers *do* react to linguistic stimuli other than those that are unpredictable. But if this is the case, on what grounds are we to base the link between the 'natural behaviour' of the reader and the linguistic structure of the message? If all responses are not taken as valid signals of encoded stimuli, that is, if only those responses which are due to stimuli that exemplify the context-contrast structure are considered acceptable, then the point of the subjective-oriented method would clearly seem to be ignored. It appears, in fact, that the criterion for what is and what is not to count as a stylistic device becomes framed in purely linguistic terms: viz. only that which exhibits a contrast-in-context structure. In this way Riffaterre's argument—that the Jakobsonian method will include linguistic structures that are, nonetheless, stylistically ir-relevant—is effectively neutralized since he admits that, in actual practice, the *archilecteur* will also identify linguistic features which, due to the absence of con-trast, are themselves irrelevant. Both theories are reduced to basing their methods of analysis on style as it is actualized in language and not as it is per-ceived in communication situations.

Stylistic structure and stylistic function

By providing precise formal criteria for the identification of the stylistic struc-ture of a message (or text), Jakobson and Riffaterre isolate a supposedly invariant relation between the formal structure of messages and a particular function of the message in communication. In the end the isolation of these invariant relations between formal structure and communicational function amounts to a definition of style (or, for Jakobson, of literariness). By determining the formal structure that a message's style must have they rule out as non-stylistic any other formal

---

[42]Riffaterre 1959, p. 170.

features of the message. Hence Riffaterre authorizes the discarding of the *ar-chilecteur's* response if the indicated stimulus does not indeed conform to the stylistic criterion of contrast-within-context. A parallel effect can be seen in the Jakobsonian postulate that only equivalence in sequence may serve as the criterion of literarity.

On the other hand, if the message seems to produce a communicational effect which to intuition might appear to be 'non-conceptual' (i.e. not 'linguistic mean-'ing'), but which cannot be linked to either a contrast-within-context or an equivalence-in-sequence structure, then that effect is not stylistic. That communicational effect cannot be explained as stemming from the stylistic or poetic function of the message, but must arise from some other dimension of the communicational relevance of the message. Even if this effect is intuitively characterized as very like 'a focus on the message for its own sake' or like the maximal decoding of the message, it still may not be seen as having its source in the stylistic or poetic structure of the message. Instead, it would have to be treated, one would imagine, as some sort of 'communicational synonymy' (i.e. two different formal structures having the same communicational function.)

The analogy is clear. Just as the bi-planner linguist isolates those features of speech (viz. expression-form) and those aspects of the communicational relevance of speech (viz. linguistic meaning) which he sees as belonging to his domain, these stylisticians, by adapting the bi-plannar method for their own investigation, isolate another formal aspect of the expression-plane and another dimension of communicational relevance as that which belongs to *their* domain: stylistics. Much remains to be explained in communication, but the linguist and stylistician say that this remainder does not lie within their investigatory and explanatory domain.

This restriction of the domain of stylistics means that Bally's goals for his discipline are no longer valued. His aim was to explain a vast array of functions of language in communication, but since his day the domain of stylistics has relegated to the category of the non-stylistic most of those functions. Other disciplines have arisen to explain them: speech act theory, register analysis, conversational analysis, psycholinguistics and sociolinguistics can all be seen to be interested in those functions of language which first drew Bally's attention. But structural stylistics, by adopting formal criteria for the identification of stylistic structure, has evolved into a discipline which Bally would probably not recognize as his own.

Why has structuralist stylistics developed in this way? For the answer to this question one only needs to reflect on the nature of the task that, since Bally, stylistics has set itself. Very simply put: stylistics—like linguistics—has always tried to explain how language 'gives' us what we 'get' in communication. Bally raised the question: how does *la langue* account for the expressive aspects of communication? Jakobson and Riffaterre altered the focus of this question to how the structure of messages accounts for their function in communication. But the assumption is the same: since (a) the structure of the message is what determines the function it will have in communication (or the effects it will communicate), then (b) the proper investigation of this function must proceed by the analysis of its source in the message. In all three cases any important role by other situational factors is denied (or depicted as merely a modifying influence). There is only one casual and explanatory equation: between message structure and communicational function. For this reason the linguist concentrates his analytic efforts on the relations between expression-form and linguistic meaning and the stylistician on stylistic structure and stylistic function. This biplanar model, based as it is on the common-sense assumption of what a language is and what a language does, cannot admit of any other sources either of communication or of the explanation of communication.

By such reasoning, both linguists and stylisticians are able to justify the construction of explanatory models which do not take into account the influence on communication of individual situational contexts. For the principle is that by reducing the explanatory claims to a precisely limited aspect of communication—such as linguistic meaning or stylistic function—other possibly influential factors may be ignored and left to other disciplines to explain. The consequences of not accepting such a reduction are clearly seen in the weaknesses of Bally's theory. On the other hand, it is not hard to imagine just how difficult it would be to isolate the stylistically and linguistically pertinent features of utterances if it *were* accepted that the meaning and stylistic function of a message does depend on various features of the particular situations of its occurrence. If the criterion by which one distinguishes pertinence is not constant but infinitely variable, no constancy of stylistic structure or of linguistic form would ever be found. And inter-subjective verbal communication could not be explained in terms of the use of a language. But the bi-planar approach simply does not allow for the relevance of any other factors other than those chosen to be explained. For, as is apparent in both the linguistic and stylistic applications of this model, the two planes are defined in relation to each other. Expression-form is the abstraction of those features of sound (or graphic) substance which are capable of creating differences of linguistic meaning; linguistic meaning concerns that aspect of the content (or communicational relevance) of speech (or writing) which differentiates between expression-forms. There is no room here for the accommodation of other influences on communication. From these other influences—defined as those which linguistics does not attempt to explain—stylistics has carved out its own similarly defined realm of investigation. No one has ever proposed a 'fundamental assumption of stylistics' such as Bloomfield proposed for linguistics; but the evolution of stylistics, from Bally to Jakobson to Riffaterre, can be seen to be working towards, or even within, such a principle. And as the lesson of Bally revealed, it cannot work without it. For structural stylistics, what counts as the stylistic structure of a message depends on what is considered to be the function of style (hence the difference between Jakobson and Riffaterre); and what counts as the stylistic function of a message is determined by its stylistic structure (hence Riffaterre's neglect of the *archilecteur's* response when it is not signalled by a contrast-within-context stimulus). Here again, there is no room to allow the influence of other features of communication and/or of situation. Riffaterre's decision to rule out the 'content' of the reader's response as well as his belief that only a stimulus encoded into the text could be the source of this response are both perfectly understandable within such a model. He could not have argued otherwise without entailing the rejection of the model.

But for Riffaterre, this amounts to rejecting the principles of his own theory on the grounds of their unadaptability to the rigours of scientific method. This rejection was inevitable since it is, in a sense, 'encoded' in the underlying principle of his method: the separation of stimulus and response. This separation is justified by the notion of the parallel unidimensionalities of reading and unpredictability. Heightened response is seen as *necessarily* caused by an unpredictable stylistic stimulus. Hence, an analysis of potential stimuli, i.e. of the linguistic forms of a message, is sufficient to predict the responses to those stimuli. Use of the response is therefore superfluous. By the separation of stimulus and response the reader's role in the perception of style is reduced to that of mere localization; and in the final analysis, even this is rejected as a popular 'illusion' of atomistic stylistics. The result is the phasing out of the *archilecteur* 'at an advanced stage of analysis' and the primacy of the contrast within context structure as the determinant of style. It was inevitable that, in spite of Riffaterre's arguments supporting a view of style as being a subjective construct dependent on the perception of the addressee in the communication situation, his respect for the scientific appearance of linguistics could not allow subjective response a greater role in the analysis of its stimulus.

5

Generative Stylistics and the Stylistics of Processing Strategies

Affective stylistics is still a vital force in contemporary thought on style. To the observer, this might not be readily apparent, and for good reason. For a few years now, Michael Riffaterre, the founder of the approach, has ceased to expound (in print at least[1]) the tenets of affective stylistics. Recent works on style contain few references to Riffaterre's theory as it was formulated in his early articles. Still, the fundamentals of his reader-oriented perspective, stripped of their behaviourist implications, have recently inspired a major new development in stylistics. This new form of affective stylistics is most comprehensively represented in a book, published in 1978 by George Dillon, entitled *Language Processing and the Reading of Literature*.[2] In this book Dillon advances the progress of affective stylistics one step further. He argues that, in order to be the scientific discipline it hopes to be, stylistics has to develop a precise, explicit model of how the reader reads.

> The way a writer chooses to frame sentences and place their elements does affect the reader's cognitive processes in predictable ways which analysis can explicate, but via the strategies of processing: a particular construction or preference of a writer is important insofar as it affects processing of the text. In this way, stylistics becomes concerned...with the way texts and readers act on each other.[3]

Only when we know more about the complex mental mechansim with which the reader 'processes' texts will we have, according to this new version of affective stylistics, a clear idea of how texts do more than simply communicate linguistic meaning. We need to be able to characterize with accuracy the precise ways in which features of the expression-plane of a text interact with and affect the reader's mind. On the basis of such knowledge Dillon hopes to found an empirical analysis of the experience of reading literature. This goal is strikingly similar to Riffaterre's earlier designs for a reader-oriented approach to style.

---

[1]Riffaterre has published a great deal since his *Essais de Stylistique Structure* (1971). But there is little mention in his recent work of his behaviourist-based theory of affective stylistics. Instead his analytical method has become more eclectic. I have concentrated on the earlier work because it pursues a theoretical analysis of style and reading while the more recent work consists of practical
[2]Dillon 1978.
[3]Dillon 1978, p. xvii.

Before undertaking a detailed examination of this new form of affective (or 'processing') stylistics, it will be necessary first to consider the stylistic theory which interrupted the continuous development of the affective trend. This was generative stylistics which, for a short period in the sixties and early seventies, completely overshadowed Riffaterre's reader-oriented perspective. This perspective was not revived until it became quite clear that the generative stylistic proposals were not only inadequate but constituted a backward step in the development of modern stylistics. A perspicacious analysis of the transformation Dillon performed on affective stylistics must take into account the reasons which led to his revival of that approach. These, in turn, lie to a great degree in both the fundamental principles and the inevitable limitations of generative linguistics.

Deep Structure, transformations, and style

In the late 1950's during the time that Riffaterre was developing his new reader-oriented theory of style, Noam Chomsky was developing a new theory of language. While Riffaterre's theory of style claimed to be based on behaviourism, Chomsky explicitly rejected behaviourism both in psychology and in linguistics. This conflict was unfortunate for the prospects of Riffaterre's new theory. For although he was presenting a theory which constituted the next logical step in the development of 20th century stylistics, he had the misfortune to couch the claims of his theory in the language of behaviourism, the *bete noire* of the new wave in linguistics. This served to pull the rug out from beneath affective stylistics before it even had the time to become established. Consequently affective stylistics never took a firm hold either in the United States or in England. Only in France, where conversion to generative grammar was slow, did Riffaterre's ideas gain any currency.

Chomsky rejected behaviourism for underestimating the human mind.[4] The behaviourist tries to give an explanation of human action which relies as little as possible on postulating unobservables. Properties of the mind are, by definition, unobservable and so are not available to analysis with the methods of empirical science. Instead, the behaviourist attempts to explain one set of observable actions in terms of another set of such actions, without resorting to the postulation of a mediating mental process. Whereas hypotheses regarding the observable may, in principle, be verified, claims about the nature and activities of the mind are not amenable to procedures of verification. Chomsky argued that the reliance of behaviourism on the objectively observable resulted in the human sciences treating humans as if they had no minds, that is, as if mental acts did not occur. He concluded that a science of behaviour which limits itself to an account of the observable can never achieve a satisfactory explanation of some of the most crucial facets of human action. One such property is the creativity of language.

[4]cf. Chomsky 1959.

Another is the acquisition of language. As a result Chomsky argued for the replacement of the behaviourist account of verbal communication with a theory giving greater weight to hypothesized properties of the mind. This is not the place to analyse the epistemological support which Chomsky provided for his mentalist theory. Suffice it to say that man's linguistic performance was claimed to depend, in large part, on his linguistic competence. The nature of this property of the mind was expressed as the internalization of the rules of a language.

It may be seen that, in fact, the mentalist re-orientation of linguistics had a lot to offer a reader-oriented approach to style. If more were known about the minds of readers, affective stylistics would have a broader foundation. Indeed, stylistics had always entertained mentalist assumptions: from Bally's notions of the expressive and conceptual aspects of thought, and Jakobson's 'focus on the message', to Riffaterre's theories about reading behaviour. The attack on behaviourism should not have included structural stylistics in the hit list. But the rhetoric of Chomskian mentalism did not encourage a rational view of the past.

It can be argued that only a mentalistic grammar can provide an adequate basis for stylistics. It follows from the same argument that the failure of pre-Chomskian linguistics to provide such a basis can be traced to its extreme anti-mentalist tendencies.[5]

In Riffaterre's case it was his behaviourist terminology which branded him as an anti-mentalist, in spite of the mentalist presuppositions of his theory. As penitence, stylistics was being asked to repent its (uncommitted) sins and adopt a new perspective, more in keeping with the puritanical methodology of generative linguistics.

A new stylistic theory was soon developed to fill the void left by the fall of affective stylistics. Not surprisingly, the new theory arose from within generative grammar. Specifically, it derived its inspirational source from one of the central tenets of the *Aspects*,[6] or 'standard theory', stage in the development of generativist thought. Stylisticians noted with interest the fundamental postulate that transformations preserve the meanings of their deep structures. What this means is that because two surface strings such as *The cat eats the moth* and *The moth is eaten by the cat* are deemed to be transformationally derived from the same deep structure, they are therefore equivalent in meaning. The fact that they have different transformational derivations (or 'histories') does not cause them to have different meanings. This is because at the start of each of their derivations lies the same deep structure, and deep structure is the source of meaning. The same would apply to the following examples:

[5]Thorne 1970, pp. 188-9.
[6]N. Chomsky, *Aspects of the Theory of Syntax*, Cambridge, Mass., 1965.

1(a). John is easy to please.

 (b). It is easy to please John.

2(a). To scream would have served no purpose.

 (b). Screaming would not have served any purpose.

3(a). He is noble to suffer.

 (b). It is noble of him to suffer.

4(a). He thought, "she has made me lie".

 (b). He thought she had made him lie.

5(a). The threads were impalpable. The threads were frail.

 (b). The threads which were impalpable were frail.

 (c). The threads were impalpable and frail.

The last two groups of examples come from an article by Richard Ohmann. This article, 'Generative Grammars and the Concept of Literary Style', was a pioneering work in the development of generative stylistics. Ohmann pointed out that, although two surface strings might be transformationally derived from the same deep structure and hence be equivalent in meaning, nevertheless their superficial difference could usefully be seen as a difference in style. Two surface strings derived from the same underlying source give the writer two different ways (or styles) in which to say the same thing.

A style is a way of writing—that is what the word means.[7]

Furthermore, generative grammar provided a ready-made terminological system for describing differences in style, that is in terms of transformational rules. Whereas structural stylisticians had always encountered difficulties in finding adequate criteria both to distinguish the linguistic from the stylistic features of the expression-plane and to differentiate between different styles, generative linguistics offered an immediate solution to these difficulties. It merely incorporated the relevant criteria in the grammars themselves. Those differences between the superficial forms of two sentences derived from the same deep structures were simply differences of style. This was guaranteed by the grammar. And it was possible to provide precise, formalized characterizations of styles. The style of a sentence would be described by the transformational rules which had been applied in deriving its surface structure from its deep structure.

Clearly, it would help to have a grammar that provided certain relationships, formally statable, of alternativeness among constructions. One such relationship, for example, might be that which holds between two different constructions that are derived from the same starting point. And, of course, generative grammar allows the formulation of precisely this sort of relationship.[8]

[7]Ohmann 1964, p. 133.
[8]Ohmann 1964, p. 137.

Ohmann examined the styles of two very different writers—Hemingway and Faulkner—and found that they differed by the characteristic use of certain transformational rules. He concluded that Faulkner frequently employed 'additive' transformations, such as the relative clause and conjunctive transformations, while Hemingway tended towards greater use of deletion transformations. Enthralled by the prospect of being able to describe and 'parse' the essential features of styles in this way, Ohmann argued that generative grammar should be adopted as the basis for stylistic investigations.

> It is my contention that recent developments in generative grammar, particularly on the transformational model, promise, first, to clear away a good deal of the mist from stylistic theory, and second, to make possible a corresponding refinement in the practice of stylistic analysis.[9]

Of course, the early developments of the transformational model were not as stable as it had at first appeared. Most unsettling for generative stylistics was the fact that the first major argument in generative linguistics, resulting in the schismatic creation of generative semantics, arose over the question of the nature of deep structure. A version of generative stylistics, based on the generative semantic revisions to the Chomskian model, was proposed by Roger Fowler in a paper entitled: 'Style and the Concept of Deep Structure'.[10] Fowler argued that Ohmann's intention to create a generative stylistics was well-founded but that both the syntactic structures and the 'standard theory' versions of generative grammar were inadequate for the task. For one thing, they left the stylistician in the position of not being able to relate two surface structures which differ only in the substitution of lexical synonyms. Fowler argues

> that Ohmann's stylistic model, though well-motivated from a literary point of view, is defective in so far as the grammatical model it presupposes is defective; that it can be corrected if the notion of deep structure in (*Aspects*) is replaced by a level of semantic representation which can accommodate an explicit theory of cognitive synonymy and (a) lexical and (b) syntactic paraphrase.[11]

Under the 'standard theory' (a) *I just bought a car* and (b) *I just bought an automobile* do not share the same deep structure and so their surface difference (*car* vs. *automobile*) cannot be characterized as stylistic. Yet certainly, Fowler argues, such a characterization is imperative for an adequate stylistic description. Indeed, a theory which could not take into account the difference in style

[9]Ohmann 1964, p. 136.
[10]Fowler 1972.
[11]Fowler 1972, p. 14.

brought about by the substitution of lexical synonyms would fail exactly where Bally's stylistics had very nearly succeeded.

The version of generative semantics which Fowler adopts incorporates the following revisions to the standard *Aspects* model of generative grammar.

(1) No transformations are optional. Those transformations employed to produce a surface sentence are seen as 'cued' in deep structure. Actives and passives are not, therefore, transformationally derived from identical deep structures. Instead each has its own unique deep structure with different transformational cues.

(2) Deep structure is semantic structure. The meaning of a surface sentence is determined by its deep structure. Two sentences with different deep structures, e.g. the pairs of examples listed on page 88 as well as (a) and (b) above may still be seen to have the same meaning—and hence differ only in style—if their deep structures 'express the same propositional content'. Hence differences in style are 'cued' in deep structure by non-meaning-bearing transformational variables.

What is, at first, most striking about both these versions of generative stylistics is how thoroughly they broke with the developing trends of 20th century stylistics. The progress, aided especially by Riffaterre, towards the formulation of a reader-oriented stylistics of *parole* was suddenly interrupted by the rejection of the psychological foundations on which the theory was being constructed. What immediately took its place was not a revised version of affective stylistics, based on the mentalist psychology underlying generative linguistics. This predictable development would have to wait until psycholinguists had had enough time to undertake an experimental examination of the psychological implications of generative grammar. Instead, generative stylistics, the theory which broke with the affective trend in stylistics, amounted to a return to the basics. What was central in the new theory was not the question that had dominated all the trends of modern stylistics: viz, how particular sentences and texts are able to communicate more than linguistic meaning. Generative linguists were not interested in such a question. So besides providing a ready-made descriptive formalism, all that generative linguistics could offer to stylistics was a response to the more elementary question, first tackled by Bally, about the source of the fundamental difference between meaning and style. What is even more striking to the historian of stylistics is the apparent similarity between the generative answer to that question and the answer offered by Bally. Both Bally and Ohmann located the source of the meaning/style dichotomy in *la langue*. In the context of the trend in stylistic theory established by Jakobson and Riffaterre, i.e. towards a view of style as a feature of *parole*, this aspect of generative stylistics amounted to a return to the traditional orthodoxy. Style was again seen not as a phenomenon of performance, but as part of the language user's knowledge of the structure of his language, that is, part of his linguistic competence.

What is obviously different about Bally's Saussurian stylistics and generative stylistics is that the former concentrated on how the meaning/style dichotomy was revealed in the communicational content of individual expressions. Generative stylistics, on the other hand, saw style as a syntagmatic feature relating to sentences as wholes. In this respect generative stylistics was more like the stylistics of Jakobson and Riffaterre. A further distinction lies in their concern with stylistic content. Bally proposed that the stylistic content communicated by different expressions could be specified within a general analysis of the function of language in communication. Ohmann and Fowler proposed no such analysis. They had no need. Generative stylistics was not required to use stylistic content as a criterion with which to judge stylistic differences in the expression-plane. This task was automatically accomplished by the structural description assigned by the grammar to each sentence. Generative linguistics offered a complete characterization of the style of a sentence without need of recourse to a supplementary theory of performance or of communication. As a result, the methods of generative stylistics could not provide any conclusions about what effects are communicated by style. Nor could it explain how the communication of style is achieved. Generative stylistics could merely provide a formal characterization of the stylistic features of a sentence, and then, only the features of the expression-plane. Furthermore, this characterization was nothing more than that already provided in the grammatical description of the sentence. As far as the communicational role of style was concerned, it simply had to be assumed that what the grammar designated as the stylistic features of a sentence did indeed have a communicational relevance. Without a theory of communication and/or a criterion of content, no guarantee of this assumption could be provided.

It is interesting that when generative stylisticians noticed this explanatory gap, they tried to fill it with assumptions which were also reminiscent of Bally. Ohmann and other generative stylisticians (J.P. Thorne and Roger Fowler) hypothesized that a writer's habitual use of certain transformational rules would result in specifiable effects in the reader's apprehension of the text. These effects would be reflected in the reader's intuitive readiness to label e.g. Hemingway's style as 'terse', Faulkner's as 'rambling', or Proust's as 'introspective'. Thorne argues that:

> . . . if terms like 'loose' or 'terse' or 'emphatic' (to take examples from the traditional vocabulary of stylistics) have any significance as descriptions of style—and surely they do—it must be because, like the description 'complex', they relate to certain identifiable structural properties. If this is less obviously the case with other stylistic terms it is only because the relationship is less clear, not because it does not exist. What the impressionistic terms of stylistics are impressions of are types of grammatical structures.

The ability to form these judgements is just as much a manifestation of linguistic competence as the ability to form judgements about grammaticality and acceptability.[12]

Just as Bally had claimed that stylistic effects are the result of particular elements of *la langue,* the generative stylisticians enlarged the dimensions of the relevant expression-element—from the word to the sentence—but argued to identical conclusions. That is, stylistic effects, or impressions, have their causal source in the application of particular transformational rules. Furthermore, these impressions are accessible through scrutiny of the intuitions of readers. The generativists were, in truth, no more mentalist than their 'extreme anti-mentalist' predecessors. Reasoning from their premises produced results like the following: since readers will intuitively call Hemingway's style 'terse', and since Hemingway's sentences rely to a large extent on deletion transformations, then, deletion transformations produce an effect of terseness in the reader's mind.

Of course the bi-planar reasoning behind these claims does not stem from Bally, but rather from the generativist practice of relying on the speaker-hearers' impressions of grammaticality, synonymity, ambiguity, anomaly, and so on. Still, the principle is the same as was found in Bally: viz. the study of the formal structure of language should proceed from the perspective of the function of language in communication. If reading certain texts causes readers to testify to impressions of 'terseness' then the production of this impression—*eo ipso* a function of language—must have its source in particular features of the expression-plane (or in the underlying rules which generated those features).

Reasoning such as this is a well-oiled move in the mentalist epistemology of generative linguistics. In order to render mental content (communicational effects, stylistic impressions...) accessible to observation, and hence to quell the crippling fears of behaviourism, the generative linguist is told to rely on his or his informant's verbal reports about those mental contents. In this case, the linguist is not obliged to produce a detailed theory of the mind in order to verify e.g. that two sentences have the same conceptual content or create the same stylistic impression in the language user's mind. He merely asks the language user—usually himself—if they do. The response provided by the informant is taken to be as good as actual observational knowledge of mental content. The problem with this reasoning is that it neglects the rules of usage which govern the use of terms like 'grammatical', 'synonymous', 'terse', 'emphatic', etc. Instead, it treats them as standing for mental states. In other words, the linguist relies on a surrogational interpretation of metalinguistic usage to give him a 'behind the scenes' look at language itself. But there is no reason why the use of these terms should necessarily report anything at all about mental contents, communicational effects, stylistic impressions, and the like. Proof that they do would

[12]Thorne 1970, p. 188.

require evidence that language provides automatic access to knowledge of other minds, i.e. that what we say is a mirror of what we privately experience. Thus it is merely assumed that if we say the same things, we therefore experience the same things. There is, of course, no *prima facie* support for these assumptions. Even if the mental effect that Hemingway's style produces in me is totally different from the effect it produces in you, we have both been trained to call these effects by the name 'terseness'. So the fact that we will both use that expression to describe Hemingway's style in fact tells the investigator nothing about the effect(s) that Hemingway's writing actually produces in us. Evidently, if stylistics were ever to get anywhere with the bi-planar model, it would have to know more about what really 'goes on' in the mind of readers. Listening to what the reader says went on, *post hoc*, only provides a most illusory type of evidence.

There is reason to believe that even the generative stylisticians themselves sensed the inadequacy of this explanation of the communicational effect of style. (After all Bally had already attempted such an explanation and failed.) Roger Fowler, for one, admitted that the generative characterization of the source of style only serves to answer half the questions that needed to be covered by a satisfactory theory of style.

> ... linguists may be able to provide an explanation for our intuition that 'the same idea' may be 'expressed' 'in different words'. What remains to be explained of course is the fact that different styles, different characters of surface structure, different foregroundings, have profoundly distinct consequences in the readers experience.... To understand how this is so, we need to answer my question in very precise terms: what are transformations for? To be more exact what do transformations do to us?[13]

In a sense, generative stylistics had discovered nothing at all. This is because it was unable to determine the communicational role of transformations. Generative stylistics contributed nothing in revealing that those differences in surface structure which are not traceable to deep structure are therefore not meaning-bearing. This claim was already incorporated in generative grammar proper. In fact, generative stylistics had neglected the most fundamental theme in the history of modern stylistics: that is, the attempt to explain how content other than meaning is communicated. A corollary to this is the attempt to explain the nature of stylistic content. The debate over the best version of generative linguistics for the purpose of locating the source of stylistic differences in expression does not address these topics at all.

Fowler was not the only one to notice this failing of generative stylistics. The literary critic Stanley Fish, an advocate of affective stylistics, saw the silence of

---

[13]Fowler 1972, p. 15.

generative stylistics on the question of communication as a crucial point in the argument for the rejection of the generative perspective on style.[14] In the introduction to *Language Processing and the Reading of Literature* George Dillon evaluates Fish's attack on generative stylistics.

> Fish is correct both in his description of the facts and in his identification of the critical weaknesses. Generative stylisticians never have sketched a model of how sentences are read, and lacking that model, have described connections between syntax and cognitive processing which strike others as vague or fanciful, a mixture of inspired hunch, intimation, and bald assertion in no way more explicit or insightful than traditionally based analysis.[15]

The source of Dillon's new approach to stylistics lies both in this criticism of generative stylistics and in the developments which had taken place in the investigations of the psychological foundations of generative linguistics.

The psychological reality of generative grammars

As in stylistics, the generative revolution created a temporary lapse in the development of psycholinguistics. In both cases this was due to the convincing dismissal of the dominant behaviourist paradigm. In psycholinguistics, this void was soon filled by investigations with the aim of demonstrating the 'psychological reality' of generative grammar. Those psycholinguists who were converted by Chomsky's arguments attempted to discover in what specifically psychological sense speakers of a language had 'internalized' a set of rules. If experimental support could be provided for such mentalist notions as 'competence', 'generate', 'transformations', and so on, then this would lend empirical weight to the claims that Chomsky's theory of language had more than a logical validity internal to linguistics. Indeed, the mentalist hypotheses on which much of Chomsky's arguments depend might be shown to be supported by experimental results. It is not here intended to give a detailed analysis of these investigations. But because of their relevance to the formulation of Dillon's new stylistic theory, an attempt will be made in what follows to summarize the fundamental issues which dominated their development.

Some experiments in the early 1960s were devised with the aim of demonstrating the psychological reality of transformational rules. A common presupposition was that understanding a sentence involves the recovery of its deep structure by 'working back' through the transformations which had produced its surface structure. For instance, it was assumed that, as early ex-

[14]Fish 1973.
[15]Dillon 1978, p. xvi.

periments indicated, informants took more time to interpret passive forms than their corresponding active forms because of the greater transformational complexity of the former. Similar experiments were performed contrasting left and right branching clauses with the more transformationally complex embedded forms. Again, some experimenters attempted to show that the memory of sentences is impeded when their derivation involves a large number of transformations. At first, many psycholinguists concluded that their experiments supported the claim of the psychological reality of transformations. But, as P. L. French recounts, this position was soon abandoned.

> In the early 1960s psycholinguists were confident that 'actual speech behaviour is some function of the abstract linguistic structure originally isolated in linguistic investigations' (Bever, 1970, p. 270). And, consistent with Kuhn's (1970) view on paradigms and normal science, research evidence was interpreted as confirmatory. While practically all confirmatory evidence advanced for the direct reflection of competence in adult performance could have been accounted for in terms of other (more obvious) factors. . ., such alternative interpretations had extremely low visibility until the late 1960s. Since then psycholinguists have increasingly rejected the notion that performance is in any way related to competence.[16]

In other words, it was becoming increasingly clear that, in Fowler's terms, transformations do not do anything to us.

It became apparent that many variables are involved in determining the speed with which hearer/readers process sentences. In addition to syntax, an important role was found to be played by semantic, contextual, pragmatic, and—importantly—sequential factors. By 'sequential' is here meant the question of the order in which verbal elements are perceived. Indeed, little firm experimental support was produced for the hypothesis of the psychological reality of transformations. It was finally concluded, as Dillon reports, that hearer/readers do not 'generate' utterances. Instead it was suggested that there might be a separate model for performance, distinct from the model of linguistic competence. A performance model would explain, for instance, how hearer/readers actually decode sentences. The need to provide a detailed description of this model gave generative psycholinguists 'something to do'. It all promised a new psychological foundation for a renovated affective stylistics.

One of the steps which led to the hypothesis of a separate model governing performance concerned sentences such as the following[17]

---

[16]French 1976, p. 450.
[17]for a discussion of these examples see Garret 1970, p. 55 and Fodor 1971, p. 124ff.

(1) John felt the child tremble.
(2) John felt the child trembling.
(3) John felt the child trembled.

While the reader perceives these sentences left-to-right across the page, he cannot make a decision about the meaning of *felt* until he comes to the final morpheme in each sentence. In (1) and (2) once he has seen the forms *tremble* and *trembling*, he then knows that *felt* means 'had the sensation of'. In (3) however, this interpretation is confounded by the occurence of *trembled*. Instead, in (3) *felt* had the meaning of 'believed'. It is important that the reader cannot arrive at an interpretation of *felt* until he has read the rest of the sentence. Or, if he does choose an interpretation before the ending, it may turn out to be incorrect. In this case the sequential ambiguity of the sentence led him 'down the garden path'. In this sense the reader's interpretation is always defeasible. In fact, all three of these sentences are sequentially ambiguous until the reader perceives the inflectional ending of *trembl-*. However, if they are considered as a unit, in the manner of a generative model of competence, then none of them is ambiguous.

Many psycholinguists came to realize that a model which treats sentences as non-defeasible wholes, i.e. neglecting the sequential order of perception, cannot provide an adequate picture of the psychological processes involved in language use. Even if it were granted that the rules of a competence model are, in some way, psychologically real, it still had to be maintained that in performance they are superseded by an independent set of performance processing rules. It was concluded that a specific, independent model of performance had to be invoked in order to explain how the mind comprehends language, e.g. while reading.

Processing stylistics

The stage was set for a post-behaviourist renovation of affective stylistics. Generative stylistics had been discredited for its inability to give any account of how sentences or features of sentences affect the reader. Furthermore, this inability to deal with stylistic content made it painfully obvious that its delimitation of the stylistic features of the expression-plane was dictated solely by the methodological requirements of linguistics. There was no way provided to tell if different surface structures were indeed stylistically relevant, and, if so, in what way. In addition, a new psycholinguistic model of reading was being developed, a model not based on the behaviourist paradigm which Chomsky had made so unfashionable. Psycholinguistics was even discovering as yet unrecognized ways in which features of the expression-plane could affect reading behaviour, and it was discovering more about the mental nature of communicational effects. The psycholinguistic model was ripe for exploitation by a reader-oriented stylistics.

Dillon's stylistics of processing strategies (or 'processing stylistics') focuses not on structures underlying sentences but on the surface features which the reader encounters in sequential order. What is of interest is the way in which the sequentially perceived form of a sentence affects the reader's processing of it. This is essentially the same concern as Riffaterre's, but his model was severely hampered by its reliance on behaviourist information-theory. This forced him to reduce the cause and effect model of reading to a simple binary system. Two pairs of linked alternatives were envisaged: in the expression-plane, predictable vs. unpredictable elements; in the content-plane, minimal vs. maximal decoding on the part of the reader. The replacement of behaviourist information-theory by a mentalist computational model of processing strategy had made possible Dillon's broader conception of reading behaviour. Mentalism plus computational mechanism allows the psycholinguist to hypothesize an expanded set of possible mental effects brought about by reading and, hence, to postulate a similarly increased set of formal causes of those effects. All depends, in the biplanar model, on what the investigator chooses as communicational content (e.g., in this case, mental effects in the reader). For it is with communicational content as his criterion that he distinguishes the source of that content in the expression-plane.

The processing stylistician is therefore concerned not with hypothesized transformations and deep structures, nor indeed with the source of the meaning/style dichotomy, but with the ordered processing tasks that the reader is assumed to perform in order to understand a sentence. These implicit processing strategies are believed to be organized into an applicational hierarchy. That is, the reader supposedly has at his disposal the ability to perform a series of mental operations. These may be performed on the sequentially perceived elements of a sentence in order to derive from that sentence a standard propositional structure. The ordered application of these operations proceeds according to trial-and-error: viz. if the first fails, try the second; if the second fails, try the third; and so on. The reader is assumed to work through a sentence, left-to-right, performing these operations on its elements in the order in which the latter are sequentially perceived. As he goes along he tries to formulate a propositional structure of the whole sentence. The achievement of this goal determines whether he has to continue processing, e.g. by applying operations which are lower in the hierarchy. The specification of these processing strategies is a preliminary stage in processing stylistics. With this knowledge in hand, the stylistician may then proceed to characterize the different processing strategies which the reader needs in order to understand the writing styles of different authors.

Dillon's analysis of an extract from Donne's 'Epithalamium for St. Valentine's Day' will serve as an illustration.

1. Thou mak'st a Taper see
2. What the sunne never saw, and what the Arke
3. (Which was of Soules, and beasts, the cage, and park)

> 4. Did not containe, one bed containes, through thee,
> 5. Two Phoenixes, whose joyned breasts. . . .[18]

Dillon argues that the reader will 'misperceive' the relative clause (lines 2-4) *What the Arke. . . did not containe* as the second half of a co-ordinate construction, object of the verb *see* (line 1): i.e. as *see what the sunne. . . and what the Arke. . .* However, this misperception will supposedly only last until the reader gets to *one bed containes* (line 4). he will then realize that the clause *what the Arke. . . did not containe* is really a pre-placed (or syntactically framed) object of the verb *containes* (line 4). In other words, the reader discovers that the two main clauses are to be divided as follows: *Thou mak'st a Taper see what the sunne never saw, and one bed containes what the Arke did not containe. . . .* However he cannot discover this until he reads *one bed containes* in line 4. He will then realize that the *and* in line 2 serves to join the two main clauses, and not, as at first appeared, to join two clausal objects of the verb *see* in line 1.

This difficult situation is caused by the sequential ambiguity of the clause *what the Arke. . . .* Dillon describes the readers processing strategy in such situations as follows:

> When we encounter a noun phrase following an apparently complete clause, we may look forwards for a verb of which it could be the subject while also considering whether it might belong back in the clause just processed. If for some reason the look forward does not give quick results, and if the noun phrase *could* be tucked back into the preceding clause, we tend to take this option. One reason that (the example from Donne) is so difficult is that it is hard ever to find a place in the following clause for *what the Arke did not containe.*[19]

In a similar fashion Dillon offers informal descriptions of processing strategies designed to deal with a variety of sentence features which impede straightforward processing. Included among these are 'chopped' co-ordinate noun phrases, apposition, inverted phrasal order, subjectless participal phrases, 'left-dislocation' of clausal elements, ambiguous pronominal reference, and ambiguous auxilaries. By specifying the various processing strategies which are assumed necessary to the correct perception of these sequential difficulties Dillon claims to have developed an approach to stylistics which can provide a precise and explicit analysis of the response of readers to differences in style.

> The model of reading sketched here does seem to furnish the beginning of a predictive and normative specification of response. . .[20]

---

[18]Dillon 1978, p. 48.
[19]Dillon 1978, p. 51.
[20]Dillon 1978, p. 184.

With the help of this model certain patterns in the expression-plane may be characterized according to the type of processing strategy they require. In this way, expression-structures may be classified according to the effect they are assumed to produce in the reader. Furthermore, the styles of different authors may be described in terms of the types of mental operations they characteristically make readers perform. Thus processing stylistics replaces generative stylistic descriptions, derived directly from a linguistic model of competence, with descriptions based on a theoretical model of the function of language in communication.

One advantage of this new approach, Dillon points out, is that it can serve as a basis for new investigations of the mimological potential of styles. That is, the possibility is raised that an author's use of a particular style may serve—by the mental response which the style produces in the reader—to communicate to the reader the mental state of one of the characters, the narrator, or even the author. Indeed, Dillon suggests, the source of stylistic taste may lie in our likes and dislikes for certain of the mental operations which an author's style demands of us. Whatever the justification of these suggestions, they certainly represent new avenues for the stylistic investigation of literature. And they demonstrate the harvest reaped by affective stylistics when it replaced the primitive binary theory of behaviourism with the computational models of a mechanist mentalism.

From Bally's 'stylistic effects', and the poetic and stylistic functions of Jakobson and Riffaterre, to Fowler's question about the effect of transformations, such a specification of response is what structural stylistics had always desired. The need for it in a bi-planar model of language is clear. Without it, the stylistician cannot determine if particular features in the expression-plane are stimuli or not. He cannot tell if they are relevant to communication at all and, if they are, in what way. That is, since structural stylistics in all its forms conceives of communicational content as an effect produced by a cause lying in the expression-plane, then a study of that cause must begin by specifying the relevant effect. The lack of any specification of response proved to be the crucial flaw in generative stylistics. By pushing the trend of modern stylistics even further into the domain of psychology Dillon claims to have found the appropriate model in which response, and the way in which that response is achieved, may be specified. This is the goal first set for stylistics by Charles Bally.

Stylistics and mentalism

The question which should rightfully concern the remainder of this chapter is the following: has processing stylistics succeeded where the earlier versions of structural stylistics have failed? To answer this we need to know if Dillon's specification of response has escaped the pitfalls of those proposed by earlier stylisticians. We have seen that Bally's notion of stylistic content is hampered by its purely intuitive basis. Jakobson and Riffaterre, on the other hand, offered only vague specifications of stylistic response—viz. 'focus on the message' and 'maximal decoding'—and, in any case, gave more weight to *ad hoc* specifications of the formal structure of the stimulus in the expression-plane. Whereas Bally may be compared to the phonologist who says that there must be a phonological system of oppositions and yet does not say how to distinguish significant from non-significant opposition, Jakobson and Riffaterre are more akin to the phonologist who simply asserts that the phonemes of the language are X, Y, and Z without furnishing any but the sketchiest of justifications for that assertion. What Bally's stylistics lacked a means to discover, the stylistics of Jakobson and Riffaterre did not even attempt to discover, but simply presupposed. Does Dillon's processing stylistics escape this dilemma?

A critical appraisal of processing stylistics will surely point out that the proposed specification of the mental operations underlying reading must, in the final analysis, rely on speculation. This is essentially the same criticism as was levelled against Bally's specification of stylistic values. Indeed, whereas Bally might say that a particular expression, for example, conveys 'disdain', the processing stylistician will say much the same: e.g. that a particular sentence requires 'such and such processing strategies'. Neither assertion about the communicational content involved is open to verification. Still the support for the description adopted by the processing stylistician is supposedly grounded in (1) the experimental results, (2) the intuition of the investigator, and (3) the internal coherence of the model. These will be dealt with in the following paragraphs.

The support that may be drawn from the psycholinguistic experiments on the reader's processing strategies depends on a variety of question-begging assumptions. It has to be taken for granted, for instance, that the reader's response to the sequential arrangement of a sentence may be isolated from any influence by context, motive, or extra-linguistic knowledge. Yet in principle this cannot be demonstrated. In her study of language development after five, Karmiloff-Smith describes what she calls 'the experimental dilemma'.

> On the one hand, we are all aware that if we design an experiment with all the extralinguistic and discourse cues available normally in language then the child's understanding may be due to the accumulation of interacting clues and not to the linguistic category under study. Yet if we remove all these clues, we cannot be sure that we are not dealing with *ad hoc*, experiment-generated procedures, atypical of the childs everyday behaviour.[21]

It should be evident that this experimental dilemma applies just as well to experimental investigations of processing strategies. Furthermore, the processing model which is formulated on the basis of these investigations must assume the

[21]Karmiloff-Smith 1979, p. 313.

accuracy of the interpretations of what are in fact highly ambiguous experimental results. One such interpretation concerns the significance of reaction times. It is all very well to produce results which demonstrate e.g. that syntactic framing delays reaction time. One would have to beg some important questions to conclude from that evidence that syntactic framing therefore requires the application of such and such processing strategies. The experiments alone simply do not provide observable evidence for theories about processing strategies. Indeed, the results of the experiments could be accommodated by a great variety of alternative explanations, each depending—to a greater or lesser degree—on context, personality, situation, intelligence, neural structure, and so on. The processing strategies proposed in performance models—that is, those strategies essential to the foundation of processing stylistics—make up only one of a large number of possible proposals, all of which conform with the experimental results. The results in no way single out one account, framed in terms of inter-subjective processing strategies, as the most plausible.

In fact, processing stylistics is as bi-planar as every other model of structural stylistics. Like them, processing stylistics has to specify some unobservable mental content which is claimed to be brought about by the reader's encounter with such and such feature of the expression-plane. For Jakobson and Riffaterre this mental content is framed in terms of increased attention and is supposedly only brought about by certain sequential equivalences/contrasts in the text. Bally spoke of the stylistic effects brought on by certain groups of expressions. Dillon's proposal is essentially the same as these although the hypothesized content of mental processing strategies and the supposed textual source of that content are new. In spite of the fact that his model is logically dependent on the hypothesis of causal links between specific mental operations and certain sequential features in the expression-plane, no evidence may be provided which demonstrates that the purported mental operations (1) exist (i.e. do occur), (2) are distinct from other mental operations, and (3) occur if and only if the reader encounters the relevant sequential features.

Like Bally and, to some extent, Jakobson and Riffaterre, Dillon supports his claims by an appeal to intuition. The assumption is that readers all follow the processing strategies rendered explicit by the stylistician, but that they do so implicitly.

> How, in practical terms, can readers discover what strategies they are employing? The key here is the experience of difficulty or confusion—in extreme cases, of incomprehension or miscomprehension. At such moments the strategies jam, and we can become aware of the origin of the difficulty by noting what in the text is unusual. Normally we are not conscious of choosing or using a particular strategy, but when the results of the processes fail to tally as a well-formed structure, we shift to a more consecutively organized

> problem-solving routine, constructing and weighing alternative readings. Usually this shift is accompanied by a sense of greater effort or concentration being expended. Paradoxically, we can learn about how we read simple texts by analysing the sources of our troubles with difficult ones. (. . .) I appeal to the reader to determine whether he finds the passages difficult, and in the ways described. . . .[22]

In other words, we are told to see in what ways we consciously work out the meanings of sentences which confuse us. This conscious method is assumed to be an explicit version of what we must unconsciously do all the time. A similar sort of hypostatization is recommended by many semanticists, that is, reasoning from (a) the fact that, when we are puzzled, we look up the meanings of words in a dictionary to (b) the hypothesis that every brain is equipped with a lexicon to which hearers refer when interpreting the component parts of speech. But must we assume that the way to understand unconscious and unobservable behaviour is by seeing some aspect of observable human behaviour (looking a word up in a dictionary, consciously working out the meaning of a sentence. . .) as an explicit projection of what we normally carry out by implicit mental operations?

The story that processing stylistics tells is based on a certain theory of mind. Every individual's mind is pictured as some sort of mechanical device, a computer perhaps, which takes in processes, and discharges information according to preprogrammed instructions. In stylistics, the new aspect of this model is the computer analogy.

Just as Riffaterre chose to overrule the reactions of the *archilecteur* by giving priority to his specification of the textual stimulus of a reaction, Dillon appeals to the intuition of the reader and yet chooses to ignore it if it appears to contradict the predictions of the processing model.

> . . . if a putative difficulty does not follow from an axiom of processing theory, one should be cautious about claiming that the reader will experience it.[23]

Why, one wants to ask, must there always be an assumption of first order priority that all readers read in the same way all the time? And if one argues that there is no such assumption, then what is a processing model supposed to represent? Like the other structural stylisticians Dillon seems to take for granted the principle that language 'gives' the reader what he 'gets' in communication. If a particular stimulus is encoded in the text—whether this is a structure of equivalences, a contextual contrast, or sequentially complex syntax—then this principle holds that all readers will produce the same appropriate mental

[22]Dillon 1978, p.. xxiv.
[23]Dillon 1978, p. 185.

response. We are asked to examine our unconscious to see if this mental response does occur. But then if it does not seem so, we are supposed to bow to the internal coherence of the theory. A theory which takes as its criterion of verification an unobservable mental operation is not falsifiable. Instead, the internal coherence of the theory has to be accepted in its defence. What such a self-supporting theory tells us about the way things really are is another matter altogether.

Affective stylistics may have finally triumphed over its brief encounter with generative grammar. To do so its behaviourist foundation was dropped and replaced by a psycho-mechanism just right for the computer age. Certainly seeing the reader's textual experience as a version of the computer's encounter with a punch card gives a more fashionable and a more complex picture than that offered by Riffaterre's unidimensional cline of reading. But the question of what either theory can tell us about reading, or about style, must remain open.

6

Stylistic Theories and Communication

The guiding principle throughout the development of structural stylistics has been linguistic reductionism. This principle holds that the effects produced in verbal communication have their causal source in observable features of the expression-plane. So, if it is felt that a message produces a particular effect in the addressee, the stylistician turns his attention solely to the message to discover the source of that effect. The adoption of this principle—reflected in the twin assumptions of what a language is and what a language does—produced results in linguistics. Consequently, it is not hard to see why stylisticians have also adopted this principle for the purpose of explaining other aspects of communication than those of the self-defined linguistic domain. It is this reductionist principle, however, which has blocked progress in stylistics.

In order to study an aspect of verbal communication from the perspective of cause and effect—that is, from the perspective of the bi-planar model of language—it is necessary to specify what it is we 'get' in communication. If this is accomplished, then the features of the expression-plane which are the cause of communicational effects may be identified. Bally was the first to recognize this requirement and the first to be defeated by it. Since his failure, every 'new' version of structural stylistics has attempted to renovate the investigation by proposing a revised account of the nature of stylistic effects. In each case, a new specification of the stylistic aspect of what we 'get' in communication is put forward: a focus on the message, maximal decoding, processing strategies, etc. In responding to this requirement stylistics has become more and more reader-oriented, and so, more and more a sub-discipline of cognitive psychology. Even generative stylistics incorporated an attempt to deal with the problem of specifying stylistic content. What was offered was a purely negative definition: stylistic content is not meaning. This was at least enough to allow the generative stylistic partition of the expression-plane into features which do and features which do not pertain to meaning. In bi-planar analysis there is no need to specify content any more than is required for it to serve as the criterion for the correlative analysis of expression.

The assumption that stylistic content is inter-subjective has surfaced in every new specification. This is the assumption that a message communicates the same content to each of its addressees. The content actually *belongs* to the message. This may be because of properties of the language or because of the way the addressee perceives the message. In any case the effect produced by a message is supposedly 'derived' from the features of the message. The principle of inter-subjectivity merely states that—whether because we all speak the same language or because we all perceive messages in the same way—the stylistic content derived from any one message is the same for all addressees. Were this not to be true—so the argument goes—there would be no sense in speaking of a message *communicating* at all. The notion of communication simply entails inter-subjectivity. Since we all feel that messages do communicate more than meaning, then what they communicate to us must be inter-subjective. The terms of the argument have changed, but Bally's reasons for asserting that stylistic content has its source in *la langue* are still as prevalent today. As a result, the problem remains of how to specify that content.

A variety of sources have provided support for the proposed specifications of stylistic content. However, considering the forces which impinge on any social science theory, these may be grouped into three primary types. First, some proposals have incorporated an appeal to intuition. Bally, the generativists, and Dillon have all asked the ordinary language-user to examine his consciousness to see if their accounts of stylistic effects are accurate. But the difficulty is to distinguish and describe exactly what is found. The ways we have of talking about mental content are limited, and it is impossible to check to see if what one person means by a description of mental content is the same as what is meant by another. A scientific description based on such descriptions must take a lot for granted.

The second type of support consists in references made to the 'discoveries' of related disciplines, that is, to newly developed ways of talking about inherently unobservable mental events. Jakobson's involvement with Russian formalism provided his notion of a 'focus on the message for its own sake'. Riffaterre pictured stylistic effects in terms of information, predictability, stimulus and response, that is, according to the language-games of behaviourist psychology. The most recent proposals are couched in the language and mystique of computer systems theory. In each case, a terminological framework, or language-game, is relied upon to give a coherent picture of the workings of the mind. Into this picture the notion of stylistic content is inserted. As such the particular specification of the stylistic aspect of what we 'get' in communication is bounded, buffered, and supported by the relations of mutual dependence which structure the use of the terms into a language-game.

In general, the concepts of the social sciences also receive support from empirical observation. As regards stylistic content, however, empirical observation is not possible. Only the expression-plane is open to observation. Still, this has sometimes provided indirect support for specification of what we 'get' in communication. Both Dillon and Riffaterre (and Jakobson to some extent) avoided questions relating to the specificity of their proposed contents by arguing that (what they believed to be) the observable expression-features of style would necessarily produce a particular effect in the addressee. Of course, such an argument only provides support for their account of stylistic effects if one first accepts their account of the stylistic features of the expression-plane. But the bi-planar model stipulates that one may only distinguish the significant features of the expression-plane by taking the criterial perspective of content.

The result is a rather curious cause-effect study where the cause is supposed to be observable, but the identification of the effect remains a question of guesswork, tradition, and some rather autocratic theory-making. The empirical study of how language 'gives' us what we 'get' in communication continues to be frustrated by the impossibility of analysing just what it is we all do indeed 'get'.

So it should be no surprise that such a wide variety of proposals have been offered concerning the nature of stylistic content and expression. Nor should there be any wonder at the extreme vulnerability of every new proposal. A theory which obliges every new account to base its pivotal criterion on a purely conjectural foundation cannot hope to achieve either stability or progress. The inability of stylistics to acquire academic respectability (or funding) stems directly from the criterial dilemma posed by the dominant bi-planar model.

Why has structural stylistics manoeuvered itself into such an awkward position? If one examines the presuppositions of the bi-planar model, the answer should be clear. Stylistics is forced to contradict one of its original fundamental insights. Saussure argued that, as speaker/hearers, we do not objectively observe messages. Our perception of language is largely determined by subjective criterial considerations. As individuals we perform an analysis on the message. We consider each element of the expression-plane according to certain criteria.

No structuralist, including Saussure, has been able to remain faithful to the implications of this insight. What has prevented them is the apparent necessity to explain language in such a way as to show how it can be a medium of communication. And communication, throughout the history of linguistics and stylistics, has been thought to imply inter-subjectivity. Thus, in structuralist doctrine an implicit conflict was created between the assumption of the subjective criterial analysis of the expression-plane and the assumption of the inter-subjectivity of communicational content. The resolution of this conflict supposedly lay in the distinction between form and substance. But this resolution presupposed that although we *individually* derive form out of substance, nonetheless we *all* perform the same derivation according to the same criteria and rules. That is, if the explanation of inter-subjective communication by language was to be possible, then it had to be assumed that all those who communicate in the same language must necessarily analyse the expression-plane in the same way. Communication had to be seen as the use of an inter-subjective language which systematically fixes the relations between expression and content. Consequently, the assumption of the inter-subjectivity of communication led to the dilemmas of reductionism.

In other words, a type of mental objectivity was presupposed in order that the accepted notion of communication might make sense. Saussure speaks of a language existing in the collective mind of the community. Chomsky, for similar reasons, takes as his object of analysis the linguistic competence of the ideal speaker/hearer. The expressive systems and reading models of structural stylistics involve an analogous sort of mentalist hocus-pocus for the very same purpose of explaining how content is communicable. But whenever the inter-subjectivity of communicational content is assumed, the insoluble question arises as to the specific nature of that content. Consequently, the explanation of how communication 'works' is, from the very start, sidetracked into mentalist guesswork.

What is needed is a new conception of communication, one which does not presuppose uniform inter-subjectivity and reductionism. Such a conception would need to consider that both our perception and interpretation of communicational events are heavily influenced by situational, experiential, emotional, and social factors. In short, it needs to remember that in communication we remain individuals.

REFERENCES

Austin, J.L. (1962) *How to do Things with Words*, J.O. Urmson (Ed.), Oxford.
Bally, C. (1909) *Traité de stylistique francaise*, Paris.
Bally, C. (1952) *Le langage et la vie*, (3rd ed.), Geneva.
Bever, T.G. (1970) The cognitive basis for linguistic structures, in *Cognition and the Development of Language*, J.R. Hayes (Ed.), New York.
Bloomfield, L. (1935) *Language*, London.
Bonnet J. and Barreau, J. (1974) *L'esprit des mots*, Paris.
Bullock, A. and Stallybrass, O. (Eds.) (1977) *The Fontana Dictionary of Modern Thought*, London.
Bruner, J. (1974) *Beyond the Information Given*, London.
Chomsky, N. (1959) A Review of B.F. Skinner's *Verbal Behaviour* (New York, 1957), *Language* XXXV.
Chomsky, N. (1965) *Aspects of the Theory of Syntax*, Cambridge, Mass.
Cressot, M. (1947) *Le style et ses techniques*, Paris.
Culler, J. (1975) *Structuralist Poetics*, London.
Delas, D. and Filliolet, J. (1973) *Linguistique et poétique*, Paris.
Dillon, G.L. (1978) *Language Processing and the Reading of Literature*, Bloomington and London.
Fish, S. (1973) What is stylistics and why are they saying such terrible things about it? in *Approaches to Poetics*, S. Chatman (Ed.), New York.
Fodor, J.A. (1971) Current approaches to syntax recognition, in *The Perception of Language*, Horton & Jenkins (Eds), Columbus.
Fowler, R. (1972) Style and the concept of deep structure, *Journal of Literary Semantics* **1.**
French, P.L. (1976) Disintegrating theoretical distinctions and some future directions in psycholinguistics, in *Handbook of Perception*, Carterette & Friedman (Eds.), New York and London.
Gagnepain, J. (forthcoming) *Le pouvoir dire*, Paris.
Garrett, M.F. (1970) Does ambiguity complicate the perception of sentences? in *Advances in Psycholinguistics*, Flores D'Arcais & Levelt (Eds.), Amsterdam and London.
Granger, G-G. (1968) *Essai d'une philosophie du style*, Paris.
Harris, R. (1973) *Synonymy and Linguistic Analysis*, Oxford.
Harris, R. (1980) *The Language-Makers*, London.
Hjelmslev, L. (1961) *Prolegomena to a Theory of Language*, Madison.
Holenstein, E. (1976) *Roman Jakobson's Approach to Language: Phenomenological Structuralism*, Bloomington.
Jakobson, R. (1960) Linguistics and Poetics, in *Style in Language*, T. Sebeok (Ed.), Cambridge Mass.
Jakobson, R. (1973) Postscriptum in *Questions de Poétique*, Paris.
Jakobson, R. and Halle, M. (1956) *Fundamentals of Language*, The Hague.
Jakobson, R. and Levi-Strauss, C. (1962) *Les Chats* de Charles Baudelaire, *L'Homme*, **2.**
Jakobson, R. and Georgin, R. (1978) Entretion avec Roman Jakobson in *Cahiers Cistre* **5.**
Karmiloff-Smith, A. (1979) Language development after five, in *Language Acquisition*, Fletcher & Garman (Eds.), Cambridge.
Kuhn, T. (1970) *The Structure of Scientific Revolutions* (2nd ed.) Chicago.
Levin, S.R. (1962) *Linguistic Structures in Poetry*, The Hague.
Locke, J. (1961) *Essay Concerning Human Understanding*, J.W. Yolton (Ed.), London.
Ohmann, R. (1964) Generative Grammars and the Concept of Literary Style *Word* XX (page references are to reprinting in *Contemporary Essays on Style*, Love & Payne (Eds.), Glenview, 1969.)
Osgood, C. (1960) 'Some effects of motivation on style of encoding,' in *Style in Language*, T. Sebeok (Ed.), Cambridge, Mass.

Riffaterre, M. (1959) Criteria for style analysis, *Word* XV.

Riffaterre, M. (1960) Stylistic Context, *Word* XVI.

Riffaterre, M. (1962) The Stylistic Function, *Proceedings of the 9th International Congress of Linguistics*.

Riffaterre, M. (1966) Describing Poetic Structures, *Yale French Studies*, 36-7.

Riffaterre, M. (1971) *Essais de stylistique structurale*, Paris.

de Saussure, F. (1978) *Cours de linguistique generale*, Paris.

Strawson, P.F. (1971) *Logico-linguistic Papers*, London.

Thorne, J. (1970) Generative Grammars and Stylistic Analysis, in *New Horizons in Linguistics*, J. Lyons (Ed.), Harmondsworth.

Wittgenstein, L. (1953) *Philosophical Investigations*, Oxford.

Author Index

Subject Index

apperception, 50-52
archilecteur, 73-75, 78, 80-81, 102
atomism, 76-77
behaviourism, 70, 74, 86-87, 92, 94
bi-planner model, 16, 17, 19, 20, 21, 46, 82-83, 93, 97, 99, 104ff
cognitive predisposition, 74
common-sense assumptions (about language), 7, 17, 83, 104
communicational relevance, 8, 10, 11, 12, 13, 16, 18, 44, 82, 91
connotation, 11, 67, 69
contrast-in-context, 71-72, 74, 77, 78, 80-81
coupling, 56-58
criterial balance, 10-15
criterion of meaning differentiation, 9-15, 21, 26
decoding: minimal v. maximal, 67-70, 74
deep structure, 14-15, 87ff, 97
Einstellung, 49-54
'emic' v. 'etic', 51
evocative effects, 38, 39, 49, 79
expression and content, 7-15, 16, 20, 82, 83, 106-107
expressive system (*système expressif*), 32, 34, 37-40
focus *of* the message, 49-54, 68ff
focus *on* the message, 45, 49, 50, 54-59, 69, 87, 104, 105
form and substance, 8-15, 26, 106-107
functions of the message, 44, 46, 48-54, 75-76
    expressive, 45, 46, 49
    poetic, 48-54, 55, 57, 60, 75
    referential, 45, 48, 53

stylistic, 17, 19, 65, 75-76, 82-84
'fundamental assumption of linguistics', 8, 9, 13, 15, 16
fundamental assumption of stylistics, 83-84
generative semantics, 89, 90
generative stylistics, 86-94, 96, 99, 104ff
identification, 34-36
illocutionary force, 47
informants, 2-3, 73-75, 92-93, 100-101
interactional dialectic, 22-23, 25, 27, 30, 38, 67
inter-determination of form and meaning, 8-16
linguistic meaning, 11ff, 14, 15, 47
linguistic reductionism (see also 'reductionist principle'), 44, 61, 104, 107
mentalism, 87, 92, 97, 99-103, 107
natural effects, 38, 39, 49, 79
nominalism, 42, 59
paradigmatic and syntagmatic, 54-55
parallelism, 58-59
performance models, 95, 96, 101
principle of equivalence, 55-57
principle of inter-subjectivity, 105-107
realism, 42, 59-62
recipient-design, 38, 39, 49
reductionist principle, vii, 7, 12, 31, 36, 82-83, 102, 104
register, 38
surcodage, 46-48, 55
surface structure, 14-15, 87ff, 96
surrogationalism, 24-26, 28-29, 92
synonymy, 12-13, 15, 33-34, 87, 89
transformational grammar, 14-15, 86ff
topic-evaluative effects, 39